The Moon of the Swaying Buds

Also by Gail Sher

PROSE
Reading Gail Sher
Poetry, Zen and the Linguistic Unconscious
One Continuous Mistake: Four Noble Truths for Writers
The Intuitive Writer: Listening to Your Own Voice
Writing the Fire: Yoga and the Art of Making Your Words Come Alive
From a Baker's Kitchen

POETRY
Elm
Early Work
Pale Sky
Five Haiku Narratives
Ezekiel
Sunny Day, Spring
Mingling the Threefold Sky
The Twelve Nidānas
Figures in Blue
The Bardo Books
White Bird
Mother's Warm Breath
The Tethering of Mind to Its Five Permanent Qualities
The Haiku Masters: Four Poetic Diaries
though actually it is the same earth
East Wind Melts the Ice
The Copper Pheasant Ceases Its Call
old dri's *lament*
Calliope
Who, a Licchavi
Watching Slow Flowers
DOHĀ
Birds of Celtic Twilight: A Novel in Verse
redwind daylong daylong
Once There Was Grass
RAGA
Look at That Dog All Dressed Out in Plum Blossoms
Moon of The Swaying Buds
Marginalia
la
KUKLOS
Cops
Broke Aide
Rouge to Beak Having Me
(As) on things which (headpiece) touches the Moslem
From another point of view the woman seems to be resting

The Moon of the Swaying Buds

Gail Sher

NIGHT CRANE PRESS
Third Edition
2017

Publication history:
    The Moon of the Swaying Buds. Emeryville, CA: Night Crane Press, 2001. Limited edition; fifty copies signed and numbered by the author. Out of print.
    The Moon of the Swaying Buds: A Spiritual Autobiography. Boulder, CO: EdgeWork Books, 2002. A commercial printing of the 2001 edition; subtitle added by the publisher. Out of print.
    The Moon of the Swaying Buds. Emeryville, CA: Night Crane Press, 2017. Third edition, corrected and reset.

The Moon of the Swaying Buds
Third Edition
Copyright 2017, Gail Sher
gailsher.com
Night Crane Press
1500 Park Avenue, Suite 435
Emeryville, California 94608

No part of this publication may be reproduced or transmitted in any form without permission in writing from the copyright owner and publisher

ISBN: 978-0-9978313-1-3

for Brendan

Haibun: a prose/haiku combination used by Bashō [1644-1694] in his travel diaries. On each page, the haiku (or, in some cases, the 5-lined *tanka*) mirrors the emotional underpinnings of the journal-like prose thereby deepening, focusing and stretching its implications.

I am amazed that Tosai, upon reading

> the sound of an oar slapping the waves
> chills my bowels through
> this night . . . tears

has only to say "The poet, unable to go to sleep, must be pondering over time that has passed and time that is to come."

misty rain
veils Mount Fuji
only to the eyes

Contents

BOOK ONE: *Mountains*

MUTSUKI: *the moon in which the grains of rice are set to germinate*   2

KISARAGI: *the moon of the swaying buds*   44

YAYOI: *the time of germination*   104

BOOK TWO: *Plains*

UZUKI: *the moon of deutzia flowers*   146

SATSUKI: *the moon of transplanting*   182

MINA-ZUKI: *the waterless moon*   213

BOOK THREE: *Rivers*

NAGA-TSUKI: *the moon in which the nights grow long*   223

HA-ZUKI: *the moon in which the leaves fall*   265

FUMI-ZUKI: *the moon of the heads of rice*   282

BOOK FOUR: *Sky*

SHIMO-TSUJI: *the hoar-frost moon*   334

KAMINA-ZUKI: *the godless moon*   302

SHIWASU: *the moon in which monks scurry from house to house reading the sutras*   399

Glossary   412

BOOK ONE *Mountains*

MUTSUKI

the moon in which the grains of rice are set to germinate

Like An Empty Chapel

There has always been a slight feeling of discomfort, a lack of gracefulness in my relationship with activities. During long summer afternoons, I'll lie on a cot on our upstairs porch feeling astray, a foreigner to the porch. Or I'll wander up the block to a field where I catch butterflies. There are monarchs and swallowtails as well as grasshoppers and other interesting bugs. I doze in the sun and capture one or two. The idea of catching butterflies sparks my imagination. I think, "I'll go across the street and catch butterflies," and then, while I do, I think, "It's a beautiful sunny day and I am catching butterflies." But there is a gap. I am disrupted in myself and cannot enter the activity, offer it enough of myself to make it come alive.

up
down
tiny canyon butterfly

I have a snowflake tree. Once a year it blooms hyacinth-colored balls that shatter several weeks later. This tree is on the side of our house with the neighbors whom I never see except when their granddaughter comes in her white dress and everyone gets in the car.

fondling for a moment
the morning sun—
her barren nest

I feel exposed on the front lawn and only play there occasionally. I never swing on our swings or eat at our picnic table or do anything laid out for me. Sometimes I bounce a ball against the side of the house near the driveway.

dusk:
a kingfisher's call
through the shallow rain

Our dining room is covered with thick black wallpaper. Embedded in its blackness are turquoise and pink birds. Since family rarely go there (it is saved for company), it acquires a mysterious largeness—like an empty chapel—where I love to stand and stare out the window.

empty now
my parakeet's cage
rattles in the wind

I am curious about my mother. In her top bureau drawer, she keeps a ring of keys on a rabbit's foot. Who is the person that puts her stamps in a crystal box along with beads and pieces of candy?

dovelet:
folds of pink
in your fluffy gray breast

Softly Blowing Bluestem

I have magic places. The trellis near my window supports a system of tight red buds. If it weren't for the trellis, I think to myself—a flimsy structure—the rose vines would trail on the ground.

dawn—
some pink, some blue
twine along my sill

I plan a garden. I go over and over the beds that are already in my backyard plot. I want something more exotic, more dangerous to grow, more extremely beautiful.

coiled on mud
a lily pad swirls
in the floodwater

I like to bake cookies. I like to read in my green chair and be under the covers writing in my diary. I like to knit. These activities involve my hands. I have a lot of "hand energy" that must be expressed or I feel at loose ends.

sudden squall—
I wrap my hands
around the teacup

I rock incessantly. I rock in my desk at school, I rock in bed at night. In my room I have a rocking chair and I rock and rock to a record of the Uncle Wiggley Stories (Peter Rabbit and Br'er Bear) and the theme from *The Third Man*.

> *the sea . . .*
> *its rhythmic chant*
> *over and over*

I choose an escape route. If anything ever happens and I need to get to Joyce Bloom's fast, I can crawl under our fence and run across the vacant lot, which would save me two blocks.

stalking down the slope
she vanishes in your shadow . . .
softly blowing bluestem

The Nails Through His Limbs Are Thick and Intrusive

Each day I walk to school which takes about half an hour. It is bitterly cold. Bundled up so that I can hardly move, I leave home numb in my being for lack of love or enthusiasm for anything.

low hills
gray with drizzle . . .
again

On my block lives another girl who is in my grade. I go by for her and if she is ready, we walk together. One morning her front door opens just as I approach, so I wait on the sidewalk. As she and her mother are saying goodbye, her mother leans over and whispers something in her ear. I freeze. I think, "Her mother just told her something bad about me." As we walk, I am aware that she "covers up" with chatter her secret knowledge of my badness.

shooing the buzzard
away from her chick
in a whirl of snow

The teacher assigns us a picture to draw. I cannot. I cannot think of anything to draw and I cannot draw. I sit emptily starring at the blank sheet of coloring paper centered on my desk. All the children are absorbed.

little seal calf
the sun, the spray
your sallow blubber still

Increasingly humiliated, and at the same time panicked, I sneak a look at the picture of the little girl across the aisle. I know this is wrong. Her head is bowed to her work and she doesn't notice me looking (I notice carefully). I see she is making a clown. Its hat is triangular and its body balloon-shaped. I think, "I can do that." Feeling like a thief, I begin to sketch an inverted triangle which I intend to turn into the top of a clown hat.

the shadow moves
the yearling . . .
freezes

I babysit a lot for the Georges. When the children are asleep I sit in the quiet house and absorb the presence of Jesus of whom there are several paintings. I notice the muted coloring (green and mustard) behind the fleshly glow of Jesus' body. Shocks of hair fall to his forehead while the nails through his limbs are thick and intrusive.

flipping the channel
your face—
for a split second

Lodging Among the Roots

My mother gives me the feeling that there is something unmentionable the matter with me. When she says, "Go play with your friends," I "get" from her tone of voice that this is really a suggestion about what I need to do to correct myself.

mucky river
and you—eyes closed tight—
lodging among the roots

I have to go to the bathroom. I go into a public stall and there is urine all over the floor and on the toilet seat and I cannot find a clean place to stand. I end up standing in the urine which soaks through my shoes and socks. Holding myself poised above the wet seat, I relieve myself physically, but come away feeling filthy, contaminated and wrong.

*leaving the pool—
the smell and
fissures down my fingertips*

Joyce and Marilyn Yawitz occasionally invite me over. I go because my mother gives me the impression that going over to other people's houses is what normal children do. But I dread it. They have too much of a system going what with their being sisters close in age.

righting itself
shuddering—
gently shaking its wings

Often they want to play with dolls. The dolls belong to them, are empowered by them and have a definite place in their extended family. It is clearly not my family. I am miserable amidst all these foreign personalities and feel totally left out. Joyce and Marilyn are caught up in their make-believe world and don't notice. I marvel at their enthusiasm. The dolls are just dolls to me, nothing to get excited about.

> *kokeshi[1] doll*
> *petal-features inked*
> *onto your broad, pale face*
> *what happened to your*
> *arms and legs*

---

[1] Sphere for head, cylinder for body, kokeshi dolls are fetish substitutes for murdered children.

I feel erased, as if I had carefully dressed for an important event that was subsequently canceled. My mother is all shiny when I come home. "Well, how was it?" she inquires, and I say, "Fine."

dusk—
a lone Canada goose
vanishes in the leatherleaf

Nibbling the Dresden Grass

I am a very slow reader. The words need to capture my heart, be vitalized by my heart before my mind will accept them.

oh my child
when I say "daddy has died"
you, who can't imagine beyond tomorrow
think it means
till then

I am okay in school though it is humiliating to learn after the fact that my two best friends, Sylvia Weinstein and Rebecca Silverman, have for the whole year been doing extra-credit projects for an accelerated group they were asked to be in. I didn't know about this group. Sylvia tells me accidentally one day in the library.

spider I'm sorry
even its sigh
cools & refreshes me

The familiar feeling of being excluded courses through me. I imagine conversations in which I don't take part—deciding to have an accelerated program for gifted students, test-taking by promising candidates and then a whole year of meetings with just the special people. I know that regular assignments are hard for me. I am amazed that Sylvia and Rebecca are able to do extra work, that this is known by others, has been discussed, organized, and no one has said anything to me.

> *old broom*
> *on the muddy bank*
> *wind-swept . . .*

Are Sylvia and Rebecca really my friends? Both have an air of being very much a part of something that has nothing to do with me. Sylvia's something is darker and full of sadness. As soon as we get to her block, I feel her other life come over her. I watch her walking down the rest of her street looking dumpy and old. I am never invited to her house.

without its yellow flowers
bladderwort—deflated—
splattered with mud

I am invited to Rebecca's house. I instantly sense the order, the higher way of doing things that is established and that gently includes Rebecca. She is not likely to fall by accident into some stray activity because lunch is regularly at 1:00. She seems protected yet free because her parents are very interested in her. I even feel they are interested in me by virtue of my being her friend.

monarch pupa . . .
swaddled in green
dotted with gold

Once Dr. Silverman invites me to participate in an experiment. I feel intensely honored. I am put into a room all by myself and wired up to a machine that administers tiny shocks though I don't feel them much.

frisky lady—
around the cow
across the ribgrass

The experiment begins to seem interminable. I grow bored in the chair all alone, squirm around and feel increasingly cut-off. When someone finally comes to get me, I learn I was observed through a mirrored window the whole time. I flush with embarrassment. I know enough to realize that in my boredom, my behavior deteriorated way beneath the level of ladylike. The Silvermans are so refined. I feel caught, exposed as a creature too undignified to be Rebecca's friend.

dirt-tipped, matted
nibbling
the Dresden grass

After this I notice Rebecca doesn't call me as often and later I hear that instead of going to Hanley Junior High, she will be going to a private school. I think about what this means—a private school. I realize that her parents probably all along planned for her to go to a private school at the juncture when everyone changes schools. Here again is the feeling of many conversations that affect me but to which I am not included.

rain again—
a solitary sheep
in the chocolate grass

A Heifer Slobbers the Filthy Water

One day when I am about twelve, I come home and find my mother sitting dejected in her red chair. "What is it, Mother?" I ask, horrified that the crisis one can feel unremittingly swelling in our household has finally erupted. She is crying and says what I understand to imply that everything is meaningless to her, that she has missed all her chances to be something in life and is miserable. Eventually the idea of returning to school comes up. Here is a ray of hope. "Yes, Mother, why don't you do that? That would be wonderful!" I feel nervously excited, as if everything depends on this. She says, "I would, but you know, I always get a headache when I have to read something. If it's assigned, I get a headache making myself read it."

pop!
teary-eyes stare
at the shriveled rubber

I stand there and rack my brains for an answer. If only I could but I know there is no chance. She'd get a headache. The only thing I can really do is join her in her deadness—or outdo her in her deadness, rendering her alive by comparison.

slurping the cone
I feel—suddenly—
old

Suddenly I hear whispers. Grandpa Herman is dead. He committed suicide. I go to my room and stand in front of my full-length mirror to see if I feel anything.

alone in my cabin
shadows of the moon
hidden by October rain

I stare at the elephant tree across the street. Because my "office" has its own door and my bedroom, which contains it, also has a door, I feel twice removed from the goings-on of the household. This sense of removal, of isolated me next to (they think "part of") a group with whom I have some affiliation, some caring and responsibility, becomes a formula for safe me.

an old door creaks
I doze
half listening

Unlike Herman, who is elegant, my mother's father slurps his soup and makes a mess when he eats dinner with us on Friday night. After dinner he sits in his chair with his pants unbuttoned and sometimes unzipped. I sit in "my" chair, across from him, by the radio and bowl of coffee candy my Grandma specifically places there for me.

drizzle-filled trough—
a heifer slobbers
the filthy water

I picture myself in my room listening to records and playing pick-up sticks on the floor beside my Victrola. The thin double-pointed rods topple in all directions as I, putting my cheek on the cool floor and scanning the scene from underneath, pick them up delicately, one by one.

fastening his rollerblade
a child kneels by the
flat blue lake

Between games I fondle the sticks, rubbing my hands up the finely carved wooden shafts. Their points are like the points of a brand new box of crayolas.

the mower recedes—
the smell of rain and
freshly cut grass

KISARAGI
the moon of the swaying buds

Young Damselfly

My "period" starts, which I don't understand. It seems unrelated to me. The fact that my body is changing and that I can have babies doesn't affect me. I am ashamed to be so indifferent. Everyone has spoken of it—much whispering and excitement. I feel untouched. I *know* that it's not important.

> *the sun shifts*
> *she shifts—then*
> *dives into the water*

The people in my books are important. Being in my room, organizing my clothes, and listening to music are important. I lie here wondering why I feel so displaced, why I am on a different track, why I can't put my finger on what it is about my life that is so wrong.

bloated
upturned
nudged by the other fish

I have my world, which is my room. Nothing random exists here. I understand the precise degree of fadedness on the shade of my reading lamp, the diamond stitching in my chartreuse spread, the daily mood of my zebra fish, and the minute changes of expression on the face of the plaster girl supporting the light on my nightstand. The books in my bookcase are all immaculately arranged by subject. As are the movie stars (Rock Hudson and Tony Curtis) on my walls.

young damselfly
clear-winged and swift
above the flower-laden meadow

I read *Seventeen* and imagine myself in control of my life, which to me means having a consistent and likable self-image. "I have a cocoa brown skirt, soft-colored sweaters, and oxford shoes and that is what I wear." Or "I have one or two navy blue skirts and many white blouses and that's all." Each plan appeals to me as a means of consolidation. As I stare at the girls in *Seventeen* and read the advice in its articles, I hang onto the words as if everything depends on getting this correct.

so insistent—
the buzz of the fly
trapped in the unplugged fridge

I consider my friends at school, Susie Rothman and Brenda Bierman, who are not like me. Susie actually is better than Brenda. There is something loose about Brenda—a part of her is capable of slipping into a posture that is not her own but she will make her own. She flaunts her unpredictableness, since she knows my life lacks the resources to be unpredictable.

satyr:
your darts
about the stands of Turk's cap

Susie's parents know her and give her permission to do or not do things. Susie washes her hair and I ask her how often she washes it and think maybe I should do this too.

under a pine
and mound of pine-needles—
another mound

Nancy Drew's loner spirit mirrors my own yet-unformed one. Tracking herself assiduously from the perspective of the clues in her current "mystery," she uncovers a deeper level of reality. When I recognize in George Eliot the same ability to implode the specific with the infinite, it dawns on me (not as a thought but as an impulse) to live my life this way.

instar:
ever-so-slowly
through the tangled foliage

Its Dappled Rib

I like the pause of breakfast and certain fragments of my walk to school—a particular patch of sweet fresh air or a house set back from the street in an intriguing way. And of course Christ the King with its exotic parochial climate. I like the fact that there are bells at school, that time is clearly delineated, though the bells themselves are harsh, not subtly eliciting cosmic overtones like the Zen bells in my later life that deeply stir one's primal lethargy.

night jasmine:
lighting my path
your white blossoms

I like the quiet hallways and in class the feeling of being warm and contained behind my desk. The desk itself beguiles me with its inkwell, pencil groove, and liftable surface. I sit here enjoying the softness of my short-sleeved sweater, its dyed-to-match cardigan, and the sensuous folds of my skirt pleats as they drape around my thighs. I cannot hear the teacher. Lecture and discussion are like so many buzzing birds filling the air with white sound.

summer night—
inching over sheets
my toes find a cool spot

I don't care for my tenth-grade teacher, Mrs. Johnson, who has a double chin and little to say, but she praises my paragraph, noting my effective use of "parallel structure." Her response touches something in me and I think that perhaps I could be a writer. I have never thought of being anything. I read over my paragraph. I actually don't know what parallel structure is. My use of it must come from some natural ability. I am deeply moved by the idea that I have a natural ability because I always feel so unable.

picking a slug off a tender leaf
tearing the leaf—
its dappled rib

I subscribe to the magazine *The Writer,* the action in itself carrying a certain unfamiliar yet tingly sort of professionalism. But when *The Writer* arrives it feels off, wooden and impersonal. The tingly wool of my coverlet, the pregnancy of my guppy, the coziness of my green chair all seem oceans apart from "News," "Deadlines," and "Classifieds"

thunderheads occlude the sky
at dawn, at dusk . . .
the moon's absent face

The fateful words of my father, "Oh, everyone wants to be a writer at one time or another" insert themselves in my being like a violation. My budding "identity" collapses in the face of his savvy. Of course. I should have known. The wish to be a writer is plebeian, trivial, predictable. Everyone wants to be *that*.

raising it
shaking it
then tucking it
in its
breast

Absorbing the Rain the Quagmire Sleeps

I lay in my dark room listening to the sounds of my family stirring, seeing the hall lights, knowing it is winter but I am still in my warm bed.

a fog horn blows—
the shivering gull
stays put

I lay here very very quiet, my being distilled into the sound and smell of raindrops. Gradually (the change registers on my closed eyelids) the wisps of light turn to bands of light, then to a screen of brownish-grey and finally to pale grey with tinges of what would have been yellow had it not been overcast.

absorbing the rain
the quagmire sleeps . . .
steeps in the morning sun

Like Thoreau, I too want to "live deliberately," though I need a plan—a guiding principle. His striped-down life is never at a loss, as mine is this minute, for a focal point, a nimbus.

windless day—
dangling from a web
a sliver of bark

It is important to me not to be interrupted. I find that people try to tear me away by telling me things or calling my attention to something. They don't understand that I'm aligning my inner self with a potential significant thing. Anything interrupts. The wrong book for example. I am only myself when I am reading. But I am not reading the book. The words of the book merely settle me into a place where I can read the gauge that tells me whether I can relax.

beneath a layer of leaves
in the pale light
her plastron still

I begin to study piano. My teacher's room is musty with music piled everywhere, but I like this thin old man who crosses his legs and leans forward to instruct me.

the boy dozes . . .
perched on his fly rod
a red admiral

I take the bus to his studio located in a slum midway between downtown St. Louis and the Chase Hotel. When the hour is over I go downstairs and wait for my father on the dark corner. I am cold. Dirty-looking men dig cigarette butts out of sidewalk cracks with a satisfied look. I am invisible and concentrate on my father. My father takes a very long time. I have a funny feeling that he has forgotten. I wait an interminable amount of time. I lose my ability to even picture my father remembering.

ducking under a leaf
the insect . . . motionless
in the downpour

I Fully Accept the Beauty of an Elephant Eating a Boa Constrictor Being Mistaken for a Hat

Mrs. Gottlieb's English class is very difficult to get into. Those who do form a powerful clique of ones who understand the shallow nature of the common (other class's) way of perceiving things. When Mrs. Gottlieb gives a quiz—she asks a question out loud and we write down our answer—she asks the question in a manner that suggests her perfect awareness of how above such questions we are, but still one must ask. While I am deeply appreciative of this precious opportunity, it is agonizing to be questioned about my reading. My experience with a book is not the kind to prepare me with a raft of facts to cough up on demand.

ceasing your croak—
turning to stone
beneath my examining eye

Still reading (mainly for self-connection) every paragraph twice, I approach Mrs. Gottlieb after class to say that I have a question. Her eyes light up just as I had hoped, those eyes saying "Now here undoubtedly is a special one, a curious young mind," and as they rest on me she requests that I return tomorrow as then she will have more time. I really don't have a question. I fully accept the beauty of an elephant eating a boa-constrictor being mistaken for a hat at face value. In fact I could stay on the first page of *The Little Prince* forever, requiring nothing further from the universe or Saint-Exupery than its companionship.

morning sun—
dozing on a mat of reeds
a baby snapper

I present my contrived question. Her face drops. The expectancy in her eyes, her pride in me, her certainty that I would be a new disciple, all disappear in a flash. I instantly get that I am out. She has seen through my "scholasticism" and understands irrevocably that I'm a fraud.

not hawks
but wind—
the branchless saplings dead

Mrs. Farrer, on the other hand, (from whom Tennessee Williams received an F) spends most of her time rescuing her bra strap. She has little of interest to say and she herself is not interesting.

August moon
overflowing the jar
with its wire-mesh mouth

I look at my classmates, who sit quietly. Anne Kelly, for example, with her neat and pert composure. Her skin is clear, her amber hair flawless. Her green plaid skirt falls squarely over her knees, exposing her thin legs and smudgeless saddles. I think, "I bet her parents care about her." I know there are people whose decisions are informed by a mysterious intelligence. I spot them by instinct.

one pink-white egg
nestled in the earth . . .
the moon

Gilded Yellow Bars

We drive to Parkmoor for dinner. My brother and sister and I are in the back seat. My mother is screaming at my father who is behind the wheel. My mother's voice rises and she hits my father. The car swerves. I am rigid with fear. I keep expecting we'll pull over, but my father says, "Roz, stop, stop it now" in a slightly elevated but calm voice, and amazingly she does stop. She retreats to her side of the front seat, crosses her arms and asks us to think about what we want to order in a voice that totally erases what just happened. My blood begins to flow and I am relieved to cooperate in this myth. She makes it easy because she completely snaps out of it.

snow buries
the leaf tips—
watch

While a family excursion is uncomfortable (phony), it is not as uncomfortable as her sudden rages (dangerous). No one ever refers to this incident. My father tells friends he got scratched by the cat.

carnage over
tiny bits of sun-dried shells
wind and weather-beaten

Again my mother and father are in the car with just me in the back seat. We pull up to the Tivoli Theater and my mother jumps out to get a closer look at the show times. My father watches her and then turns all the way around and faces me as if I am his best buddy. "Isn't she beautiful!" he asks in a tone of voice that conveys the selectiveness of the people to whom he reveals this opinion. My eyes automatically follow my mother. I am surprised at the level of passion my father discloses and new vistas about their relationship open up to me. His frank admiration is an entirely new twist.

gilded yellow bars—
also gleaming in twilit waters
a male's eyes

I hear a tap on my window. It is my father standing on a ladder pleading with me to let him in. I am about to let him in when I hear banging and screaming outside my locked bedroom door. "Don't you let him in, don't you dare let him in." My father hears this too and says, "Come on Gail. Let me in." My mother is still yelling and I know if I unlock the door, she's capable of pushing my father's ladder down and maybe killing him.

silent snow
silent house
I stand in the moonlit doorway

I Am Very, Very Old

The air is nippy, not warm as the lemon-colored light suggests. Wetness congregates on the cement slabs and looks like slush.

another rainy day
even the chrysanthemums
droop

I am aware of feeling old. I am fifteen but feel the heaviness of age—that my circumstance of being a high school teenager is wrong.

straggling through
the cloven ice—
yellow floweret

I am deeply humiliated at being presented as a teenager and frustrated with the impossibility of conveying why to an ordinary person. My mother, for example, doesn't understand. I don't either really. I just know that I am very, very old.

sweeping brittle leaves
the sadness
of autumn wind

I walk to the Loop and watch old ladies eat. The cafeteria is drab but I am aware of the fact that these women understand how their plain meal falls into the scheme of things. I don't have a scheme of things. I am envious as I watch them seated primly in their hats.

downpour:
the old woman spread out
in front of her t.v.

I don't understand my needs. They are so large and so age-inappropriate that I feel stranded, cut off even from the possibility of getting them met.

Midsummer night:
the feverish man
frets
over his little boy
of years ago

Smack of a Jaw, Slap of a Tail

I sit at my desk and feel hungry. It is after school and there is an hour and a half before dinner. I am not interested in my homework. This is tangible. Whereas Andy, for example, approaches his subjects with a breadth of vision that immediately accepts any new item of information, refurnishing the vision so that room is made for this or that fact, I intrinsically balk at anything not vitalized by my heart. Information is intrusive. I can't think. I don't want to think. I want to be left alone to catch the few sporadic happenings that are in accord with me.

between the cries
of a black-crowned night heron—
the sound of unseen birds

I want to eat alone. Or not eat. I become aware, through off-hand comments made by Susie Rothman, of dieting, a totally new concept. She, who is perfect, claims she is fat. I notice she always brings her lunch now and it is calibrated to make her thinner. What she brings seems pathetically little but I begin to calculate. I bring an apple for lunch and at dinner I manage to find an excuse to leave the table before finishing my meal. No one notices.

still drinking the phlox
beneath my net . . .
a swallowtail

When I eat alone I have quiet (often total silence—everyone is asleep), I am tired (at the end of a long day—I feel I have "earned" eating and I'm ready to enjoy it), I am reading (taking the edge off my inner chaos), and often in bed (warm, comfortable, safe). I have everything I want in an endless supply. If the real world is too intolerable, I change it, create my own "fantastic" setting.

bowing over
the frog's grave—
cherry blossoms

I lose weight. I severely measure my food and notice that my clothing hangs on me. The waists on my skirts are way too big. Now I mostly wear one of two navy blue ones. This is very simple and with my dark hair and thin body I feel graceful and in control.

springtime:
nubbed with buds
the slender plum

My clothes need to be quite simple, I realize, or else they overwhelm me (make a larger statement than I make). To stay larger than my clothes I need (1) to limit them in number (2) to clearly define them (to prevent them from defining me) and (3) to monitor my relation to my body so that I experience this connection intensely, rendering clothes insignificant by comparison. When my clothing hangs on me, their position as appendage is exaggerated. The statement is, "See, I can do without you. You are mere coverings to me who is the important fact." I need to do this because it's easy for me to begin thinking my clothes are more important. My mother thinks they are. She is much more concerned about my clothing and makeup than she is about me.

chiseling your limbs
your leaves . . .
the hollow wind

My mother says if I don't wear lipstick, I can't go places with her. I feel messy when I wear lipstick. It's always coming off and I have constantly to worry about freshly applying it. It takes over my face, whereas I want my own face. I am hurt that my mother doesn't.

smack of a jaw
slap of a tail . . .
silence

I am reading in my green chair. My mother comes in to say something to me but instead looks at me and begins screaming, "Look at you. Look how thin you are. Look at this" and she grabs my pencil-thin wrist in disgust. I say, "I'm fine, Mother. I'm not that thin. I feel fine," but inside I fear her. Deep down I know I don't have a leg to stand on because while I am much too thin, I need it to be this way. My life depends on my ability to keep it exactly this way.

more strikes
and afterwards . . .
swirling pondweed

In the Barber's Pole Gyrating

Summer days are long. I sleep late then lounge on the beach. The friends I have all have jobs (belong to something), which underscores my nonbelonging. I am sensitive to this on the one hand and am to some extent embarrassed by the ultimacy of my availability. On the other, there is a relieving honesty about it, nonbelonging being such a reality for me.

whirling with the tide
in the shallow's
flattened stubble

When Danny visits me he hunches over as if apologizing for being visible. Ordinarily he flanks himself with a moderate-sized protective system: first, his buddies in Delray, then his fraternity at college, then his "class" at medical school, and finally his circle of elitist friends at the University of Chicago. In each case the groups are delineated, know him well, and function as an extended family. Each exerts a value structure and behavior code providing a context, a kind of ersatz self-reference. Like a musician playing with a band, his own voice, while distinctive, is mellowed out, augmented, and in the end enriched and strengthened by the presence of others—the solution of an extrovert.

wading in the pool
long black legs—and more—
long black legs

Danny has said he will write to me during the winter, but makes it clear that he will not write love letters. Wanting his letters on any terms, I acquiesce. A letter from Danny means "Dear Gail Sher" followed by the weather followed by newsreel. Interspersed are witticisms or turns-of-phrase that say everything about his caliber, his sense of timing, his gentle eye and funniness. In his hands everything (me?) is viewpoint which becomes objectified (articulated), thereby enlivened.

muscle-shirt, spiked orange hair
in the barber's pole
gyrating

Indeed he writes to me every week, which is really like writing to me every day because every day the reality of a possible letter from Danny dawns on me as I enter my house and either consumes me if there is one or fills me with hope and rationalizations if there isn't. Coming home from school means coming home to a letter from Danny not yet manifested or a letter from Danny in a blue envelope with "Miss Gail Sher" written in his tiny intelligent hand.

winter sun—
pale wings
flutter about the woodpile

I have so internalized Danny (my projections onto him) that I understand myself only insofar as I make sense in his eyes.

giant redwood:
storing the sunset
in your luminous trunk

A Trefoil for St. Patrick

One day I get the idea (probably from my mother) that it would be nice to invite Danny over for dinner. Until now we have either gone to a movie, for a walk by the ocean, or (my favorite) a moonlight swim. Occasionally, if we are with his gang, we play volley ball on the beach or hang out somewhere. My asking him over for dinner thus is quite a departure 1) in kind of activity and 2) in my being the initiator.

summer fades—
a patch of seaside daisies
waves in the salty air

I put my entire soul into the planning and preparation of this meal. I know it means Danny's first insight into domestic (wifely?) me. To be safe I choose something extremely simple (hamburgers) to make. Everything is ready when first Danny is late and then the phone rings and Danny says (to my mother) that he is on a friend's boat and can't get back, he'll have to come another time. I immediately have a fantasy of Danny on some luxury boat, suavely dressed, suavely flirting with many suave (sexually sophisticated) women, far away (since he can't get back) from incapable me. Suddenly it all feels very wrong. Inviting him, pretending I can cook (the hamburgers seem ridiculous), pretending I can in any way satisfy him.

minnow in its beak
young crane stops
in the rippling bog

Both relationships and intellectual pursuits have failed to anchor me in such a way as to promote a true connection, one that requires loyalty for example. I feel loyal. I feel in fact that I am too loyal, that my desire to be devoted to something flails around, latching arbitrarily onto this laundromat or that hair stylist so that I can't help but notice the inappropriateness.

twinkling sky—
bouncing on her bosom
a trefoil for St. Patrick

Since Thanksgiving Danny has not written and when I get to town at Christmas he tells me he won't be able to see me much (very ambiguous). It is the end of the evening and we are standing as if we were going to kiss but instead he tells me this, very softly.

night falls
shadows
under fluttering wings

My feelings of desolation are all jumbled up with feelings of disgust upon seeing my father sitting in the living room with his testicles bulging out of his bathing suit. He (my father) is wrong here and now "here" feels terribly wrong.

sliced by the squall
wings litter
the dirty sand

Danny is seeing Lorna. The whole town is aware of this since Danny is being very ostentatious about it. The picture of Danny heatedly pursuing anyone makes his little proclamation to me (which carries the implication of "circumstances beyond his control") forced and silly. Here is a world that excludes me so thoroughly I am surprised he remembers me enough to make an excuse.

"Crook, Crook!" he cries
then ceases abruptly
when it's over

YAYOI

the time of germination

Vapor Rising Over Just-Stirring Birds

Mrs. Mahaffey, flabby, scattered but good-natured, owns a cardboard box, two of whose rooms she lets to University of Florida students. Linda has one. She is a first-year graduate, sweet, uncomplicated, generously giving of her time to help with the perpetual stream of crises emanating from Mrs. Mahaffey or one of her two kids. "They did lose their father less than a year ago," Mrs. Mahaffey, teary-eyed, reminds us day after day.

summer wanes . . .
    on the windy tableland
        the sough of whistling wheat

My tiny room is next to Linda's tiny room and kittycorner from the bathroom. What stands out for me, however, is neither the crampness nor the shabbiness so much as the possession of a piece of land. Never mind its size and dilapidation. I have a bed, a chair, a record player, a closet—everything I need.

monarch:
its soft whir
in the mountain air

Linda helps Mrs. Mahaffey cook and joins the three of them for dinner and sometimes breakfast. I am not interested. I am interested in undistractedly pursuing literature and music or, more accurately, to anchor my need to devote myself to something. This need rules the gamut of my decisions from professional development to shaving cream. If I can latch onto something, I am quieted. At least a part of me is. The other part, lost in an incomprehensible sea of confusion, aimlessly treads through day after day. There is almost a poignancy in the futility of my efforts, which I do not see—neither the poignancy nor the futility.

male on nest—
his cry
in the rising meltwater

I ride my bike to the student cafeteria. The staff is still getting organized and the few other students silently absorbed. I feel very "alone in the presence of others," as if all those with the same preference for early morning make up a family of sorts, that this is tacitly acknowledged, and we all agree to ignore each other. It feels like a little club—to me—because I need to belong to something. The cafeteria is warm. There is food, light, and the sense of people preparing things for me.

daybreak—
vapor rising over
just-stirring birds

During the day I do what I can but I don't entirely understand the nature of my energy cycles and waste a lot of time. Though I go to an eight o'clock class, from nine to twelve I am dizzy and ungrounded. At noon I eat lunch, attend an afternoon lecture, and run errands. By five the day that had dawned so promisingly has seen not only nothing remarkable but almost nothing at all.

lowering sun . . .
a few red leaves
blaze in the flaccid grass

The Slender Stem—Flowerless

I say I want to study literature but really I want a home. Books do it. The problem is only certain books, a fraction of the ones required for an English major. Those that don't, don't—"it" being grip me in a way that immerses me despite my mind. Because my mind is not available. It has the full-time job of managing the fact that I do not feel seen or loved for who I am.

pale, grey
the slender stem—
flowerless

Plus I have larger questions about my intellectual capabilities. If I don't have a "fine mind" does that mean I'm a worthless person?

staring at the second egg
tawny chick—
still

In one class I am required to write a paper. I have no idea what to write and am foreign even to the concept of critical thinking. Shortly before the paper is due I stumble upon the phrase "dialectical materialism." My mind cannot fathom the real meaning of this term but the words themselves strike my fancy. I enjoy the sense of their elusiveness. The a's, i's, and l's are clear and bell-like (as in my name).

cold snap:
riding a tailwind
a male skipper

I allow the fact that I don't know what I'm talking about to become secondary to the fact that I use this expression in many sentences. I make some valid points having to do with side issues. When I turn the paper in, my sense of satisfaction is undermined slightly by fear . . . of fraudulence, of not knowing what I represent myself as knowing, of being found inadequate, or worse, untalented.

more than wind
more than cold
rustles through the stiffening reeds

On Hunter's Soil

I feel snug in my airy room in a twenties wood-frame house, very Evanston: sheer breezy curtains, rocking chair, desk, bed, and throw rug. I sit in the rocking chair and look out the window. I read in bed. But I only feel contained when I am eating.

scattered seeds—
on hunter's soil
a crane

I get up and walk several blocks to the campus cafeteria. Its wooden booths enclose me in my world of books, which I ingest along with donuts—very intent. I feel alive, thoughtful, capable of knowing whatever it is I need to know. Maybe I read five pages.

vigorous air, hard bright sun
flood my window—
rousing me

When I get to class I am overly conscious—thinking "Here I am in the class"—as if this were the important thing. Because I can't be in the class (my psychic energy is inextricably bound up in quite different matters) I can only have a sense of how it would be if I could. A phantom student, I proceed through the day, returning to myself, refurbishing myself, encouraging, cheering on my ghost-act (and stifling any inklings of awareness to this effect) at mealtimes.

darker
colder
each day
arcing
lower

No one from Northwestern lives in my part of town. I live illegally, unaffiliated. If discovered I would be expelled.

her solo
pierces
the winter sky

In one course there is a woman who always sits in back. She is fat and looks uncomfortable in her body. I stare at her. I feel a bond, a deep connection . . . probably because my situation too is out of control.

cold air sinks—the hollows
a black network
of bare
elm

I begin to eat compulsively. I read and eat candy bars after which I feel starving. I eat grilled cheese sandwiches. I feel cluttered and weighed down. I know I don't have a grip on my eating but, lonely and afraid, I feel increasingly compelled to eat in a destructive way. Food renders me unconscious, as my eyes scan the unintelligible lines of *The Faerie Queen* and page upon page of pre-Renaissance drama.

mosquitoes
mosquito-flies . . . bloat
the stagnant water

My pattern is to read, worry over the material, and make straight C's. Most of the exams are three-hour essays. My mind goes blank as soon as I read the question.

breathless, the trekker stops
places another stone
atop the icon's little pyramid

One day it occurs to me to write my "answer" before I arrive at the test. I figure the teacher basically wants to see if we have a consistent, supportable thesis. I can't come up with one under pressure but, using my imagination, I can think up one that will match a likely exam question. So I do. Instead of rereading plays with hopeless inattention, I develop an argument and organize an essay and even take notes inside the cover of my bluebook. These notes represent the sum total of all my knowledge. When I get to the test, whatever the question is, I relate it to my answer. From now on I get all A's. The teacher is always amazed at how cleverly I weave in something he hadn't quite expected.

now
after they're gone . . .
their ceaseless cries

Abode of Snow

The soft plucking of a banjo awakens me. Peeking through the venetian blinds I watch both sky and land gradually redden even while being glossed in a coat of white.

tall and still
the shadow of a deer
in the moon-drenched pines

Wind-driven snow rattles the glass. As each flake strikes, instead of melting and dribbling down in a little rivulet, it adheres to a layer of frost that is forming on the windowpane. Treetops, gabled roofs and rolling lawns relax under a blanket of softness.

drifting
        then dissolving . . .
                delicate snowflake

Snowflakes twirl through the air, coming to rest on my cheeks, and nose and mouth. Unlike rain, or even drizzle, which angles steadily downward, snowflakes ramble, drifting from the sky.

wind-driven snow
and you—oh white bird
bouncing, leaping
treading air
in the squall

Along with memories . . . fat glass bottles huddled under a collar of white, the tabbed bottle-tops and pleated caps crisply hugging each neck—(I'd jimmy open the door, grab the bottles by their throats and lug them inside two at a time) . . .

her breath stops—
the frozen moor
covered with night

Powdery snow has already reconfigured the little trail carved by my boots. I tilt my head and open my mouth to taste some of the icy flakes, then shut my eyes the better to exude my consciousness into the random bits that startle me.

moonlight:
your carmine glow
among the saplings

A usually-muddy footpath drops down to the lake. Snow melds the path and the surrounding property so that there is only one expanse of virgin hill broken by an occasional house or tree. The lake itself looks like a meadow.

pine needles laced with snow—
between their clusters
your departing V

Fingering the Parched Riverbed

I love the words of Chaucer. Every line is packed, I feel, with energy, poignancy, an undertone of double-meaning—restrained yet exuberant. I want to hold each word, to cherish and sink into each word.

fingering
the parched riverbed
trickles . . . then rivulets . . .

The nature of middle English, guttural, dignified, lofty, though innocent in its primitive development, moves me to the core. I read *The Parliament of Fowls* and *Troilus and Criseyde.* I read *Piers Plowman* and *Sir Gawain & the Green Knight.* The details of an allegory for me are not the point. The way the thing is said, not the thing itself, is what is important.

funeral over . . .
down frozen cheeks
driblets of rain

It is increasingly obvious that I cannot perform the feats of the average graduate student. There is a sense of impending doom— it is just a matter of time before the cumulative effect of my inabilities become decisive. I sit on my Berkeley couch, book in lap, and stare into the fire.

dusk—
a small green bird
flits to another branch of the seedling

Your Rattling Wings

I have on a plain, navy blue woolen smock. I have my very long hair and intense interest in the texts we are going to study. Arthur claims that when he first saw me seated across the seminar table, he went home, decided to marry me, then asked me out for coffee. I probably looked the picture of promise.

on a tuft of moss
near a flowering cranberry
eggtooth intact . . .

We are given a booth for two. I am glad to be here though I am not interested in Arthur. "It's okay to be doing this even if you don't care for him," I tell myself. In fact there is something exciting (almost dangerous) in behaving the way a normal person would. I order a hamburger and salad (which I know will make me bloated and soggy, ruining my energy for the rest of the day). Arthur is simply using the means at his disposal to get to know me. But I am not I outside of my "environments." I am definitely not I eating non-I foods. (At the time I don't have any of this figured out.)

across her nest's sandy ridge
dragging her spiked
inch-long tail

I feel radiant, stimulated, charmingly present. I'm sure I succeed in further intriguing Arthur who is there because he really cares. I am there for the exhilarating experience of pretending for an hour that I could possibly be the person he has in mind.

despite a fever
reading the sutrā
in the rainy dawn

Arthur lives alone. His "bungalow" of ivy-covered cobblestone has a fireplace, marble floors, and medieval door. The seven dwarfs might have lived there. It is in a court of ten to twelve similar bungalows facing each other instead of the street so that from the street one sees a little path of stepping stones leading—it is unclear where.

dusk
        at the canyon's lip
                pauses

Inside he has a painting. There is a moon with some colorful figures by a Mexican artist. Arthur knows that the University library loans certain works of art that they lack room to display. He gets in line at 6:00 the previous night and sleeps in line so that at 8:00 a.m. he has first choice. I am deeply moved by the painting. I am deeply moved at Arthur's passionate act to acquire it. Arthur seems so clear about what he wants. And, I think, what he wants is exceedingly fine.

landing on a spear of rush
bending the rush—
    your rattling wings

Fast Asleep in the Silver Birch

Our cozy apartment with its high ceilings and bay window feels lavish. One wall holds a library. Two are covered with burlap drapes whose pinkness enhances the pinkness in a Gauguin print. I never feel alone. Whenever I am here I feel amalgamated.

burning off the morning haze
a sunbeam spots
the tip of her nostrils

Our favorite place is a Japanese home-style restaurant called the "Hou-Kou." It feels very quaint and restful sitting here before a curtained window, hearing plucky oriental music and being served a meal that we semi-cook ourselves. A hou-kou is a tiny cauldron with a lid and its own little burner. The owners of the restaurant light it, fill it with shiny noodles and a delicious broth, and bring us a large platter of carefully chopped vegetables, fish, tofu, and so on, which we briskly dip with our chopsticks into the simmering liquid.

circling the cove
immense blue wings
stir the stagnant ether

I eat my meals at an oaken table with straw placemats and dark blue crockery. I rest in my Morris chair. Surrounded by books, rich textures, colorful paintings, thoughtfully prepared food, I am trying out a person I can possibly be. But it is too laid out for me. I am me because of a concept of my mother's. (This is unconscious.) So nourished am I by the vibrations of this fantasy, that I think (I actually believe) I am me.

twilight . . .
fast asleep
in the silver birch

BOOK TWO
Plains

UZUKI
the moon of deutzia flowers

Monotony, Both Lugubrious and Strangely Crisp

The first moment I enter a *zendo* it feels right. I have hardly heard of *zazan* but as the sun rises and I chant the Robe Chant, this gesture feels correct. The same sense—almost a nostalgia—comes over me at *teishō*. Katagiri-sensei's words grab my being as if gently shaking and then opening it. This is real. This is so. And while the effort Zen practice requires seems almost beyond my capabilities, the freshness, the certainty of inner knowing, compels me again and again to greet the dawn with a straight back.

home at last—
I sleep
numbed by rain

The room is dark and fragrant. People are getting settled, plumping their cushions, and swaying back and forth. Seated along a far wall, I quickly become absorbed in the vibration of bells and silence reverberating into one another.

one plum falls
a warbler's screech
in the distance

Meals, finally, bring warmth. It is clear food, straightforward food I respect. Then more sitting, a lecture, tea with a surprise sweet. I find the rhythm akin to me. The monotony, both lugubrious and strangely crisp, washes over my being, very familiar.

moonrise—
a silhouette drifts
along the inlet

Still, I can't adjust, get comfortable, find the right posture. The day takes forever. Its elegance, which describes a frank and beautiful way to be, becomes an injunction by sheer force of its multileveled presence. I find myself acquiescing, agreeing almost as an aesthetic response. But I am cold and scared. Actually the Buddha (the *Tathāgatha*) often appeals to this bony migrant aspect of his disciples.

a shorebird cries—
across the dunes
the hollow rattle of wind

Dark Wet Mud

People sleep. All but a *doan* who lights the lanterns and then stomps through camp ringing the wake-up bell at 3:20 precisely. Thump thump thump. The fact that the bell is hand-held, hand-rung (a human being is running, swiftly, steadily) softens the effect of its clangorous sound. Suzuki-roshi says, "When the wake-up bell rings, get up. Never make a decision twice." I snuggle more deeply into my sleeping bag.

silence . . .
but for buntings
twittering in the sedge

My mother is dying. She is lying beside a swimming pool in a down sleeping bag. I bend to pick her up (she is so light, so light). "Oh mother, don't leave!"

*Christmas:
our lawn
solid white*

The effort that it takes to get up, wash, dress, walk through the rain to the *zendo,* seems out of proportion to the accomplishment. Lonely, tired, cold, knowing exactly why I do this, I wonder why I do this.

kerplunck—
scurrying through the grass
then plopping in the water

Monastic life has been known to me forever. I am back now and the simultaneous feelings of freshness and familiarity pass over me in waves.

home at last
not a single leaf
on the crooked tree

I am given a room with two "older" students in the barn. Indeed with their altar, scrolls and vases of flowers they seem delightfully snug. I have no possessions. This is an appealing concept and represents a shift for me, but I can't relax.

no ducks, no geese
just snow
on the frozen lake

My drab corner mortifies me. I have nothing to soften its impersonal coarseness so I end up with no place of refuge, no solacing activity. Before I arrived, I had my rocking chair, my books, my harpsichord. I had food I chose myself, I had a companion, I had the presiding thought of devoting my life to music and literature. Now I have the stricture, "Everything I own I carry in my backpack."

traipsing in my getas
down the rain-drenched path
a single squawk
through the darkening
morning air

The barn is at the outer limits of the monastery grounds. It bothers me that I have to walk so far in my unsteady shoes on the unsteady path, sometimes in the rain, often in the dark. People who live in the dorm, I think, get to hop next door, whereas I have to trudge my way gropingly, clumsily, allowing an extra fifteen minutes. I see this as significant. It falls to me to work harder, to have to get up earlier, to arrive with my shoes caked with mud or soaked with rain—and to have all this unacknowledged.

afterwards
what's left of her tears—
dark wet mud

For Our Sakes the Clams
and Fish Give Themselves Unselfishly

Morning *zazen* ends. The bell rings (the *shijō* once) announcing the transition to morning service. We place our *rakusus* on our heads, chant the Robe Chant, let down our *rakusus*, then fluff our cushions and line up in the aisles for prostrations. After the bowing we reseat ourselves, this time in *seiza* facing the altar. Thump thump thump thump. A loud *keisu* punctuates the *mokugyō's* steady beat.

Avalokiteshvara Bodhisattva, practicing
deeply Prajña Parāmitā,
Clearly saw that all five skandhas are
empty, transforming anguish and distress.

As morning service concludes, the head server strikes the *umpan* announcing breakfast. *Zendo* students return to their cushions, this time facing out.

Buddha, born at Kapilavastu,
attained the Way at Magadha,
preached at Vārānashi,
entered Nirvana at Kushinagara.

A roll down on the *taikō* (Great Drum) begins, slowly at first, while the head server approaches the altar, tray (containing three tiny bowls with the three foods we will be eating) held high. The drum roll picks up speed as she nears the dais, gains even more momentum as she ascends its few stairs, and peaks as she bows and offers the tray to the Buddha. She bows again and retraces her steps according to which (her relative distance from the alter) the drummer calibrates the intensity of his beat. It is downy at the end, a hum before the final boom. Then the Roshi is served while a team of servers approach the students by twos.

Now as we spread the bowls of the Buddha Tathāgatha
we make our vows together with all beings;
we and this food and our eating are vacant.

Chanting continues while the servers serve. With pot at eye level a server bows between the first two students, kneels and begins scooping food into the first person's Buddha bowl (the largest of the three nested ōryōki bowls). A slight lift of the student's upraised left hand (her right hand holds her bowl) signals the server to stop. The server serves the second person, then stands and bows again between the two as they, bowls raised to eye level, bow in return. This procedure is repeated until everyone has food in all three bowls.

First, we consider in detail the merit of this food and
      remember how it came to us;
second, we evaluate our own virtue and practice,
      lacking or complete, as we receive this offering;
third, we are careful about greed, hatred and
      ignorance, to guard our minds and to free
ourselves from error;

Reciting the sutra forces us to incorporate ("take in") the tremendous significance of ingesting another being, transmuting its nature into actions that we deem worthwhile. "For our sakes the clams and fish give themselves unselfishly!"

> *fourth, we take this good medicine to save our bodies*
> *from emaciation;*
> *fifth, we accept this food to achieve the Way of the*
> *Buddha.*

The words bore into my heart as I, Buddha bowl cradled in my raised fingers (the thumb and two fingers from each hand create a miniature platform), intone them along with everyone. The privilege of being here, being served with others, the enormous unlikelihood of this opportunity given the millions of lifetimes of multifarious effort needed to create it, overwhelm me. I am filled with awe, and respect, for myself and all sentient beings whose combined consciousness make this rare moment possible.

Bashō
with ears so finely tuned
how could you miss
the screams
of the chestnut
        moonlight
        the sound
        of the burrowing worm

Two minutes ago I was harping (mentally) on how tedious and unnecessarily dragged out our meal ritual is. Day after day the same motions, the same sounds, the same sort of food. "Just let me eat my peanut-butter sandwich in peace" (I rail on inwardly). The opening words of the *sutrā* jolt me back to the state of mind that originally brought me to this monastery. I chant them with relief. Thank God (I say in my un-Buddhist manner) I had the sense to place myself in circumstances that would oblige at least my body and mouth to act with wisdom. Were it not for the help of this community, I *would* be munching on my peanut-butter sandwich full of desire and confusion.

> *one bolt*
> *searing the landscape*
> *white*

The shift is instant. Gratitude wells in mid-sentence. Yes. After all, this is the correct understanding. It did take innumerable labors to bring me this food. I *should* know how it comes to me.

moon-viewing kinhin
gazing with one face
at the dark Halloween sky

Oh, All You Hungry Ghosts

Chanting ends. Eating begins. First with the contents of the Buddha bowl, the centerpiece of the meal. Items from the second and third bowls are interspersed as condiments. One picks up the bowl from which one is intending to eat, takes a bite, chews the food, then replaces the bowl before picking up the bowl containing the food destined for the next bite.

from blade to blade
picking seeds
from the toppled reedgrass

Food. A monastic preoccupation. The emotional part of eating goes haywire. Many are new to a vegetarian diet. However much the *tenzo* (head cook) might wish to placate the *zendo* students with a baked potato in the Buddha bowl, how is she going to manage the sour cream, butter, chives or bacon bits that westerners expect with it—(condiments are awkward to serve in an ōryōki-style meal)? Unlike the Japanese, for whom such foods have an almost spiritual significance, Americans are not satisfied with polished rice and *umeboshi* plum. Tofu is not steak.

chicks shrieking
in the predawn light . . .
o mother swallow

Eating is deliberate. Each dish features its own flavors and textures unlike the western style of piling onto one flat plate several foods that blend into each other. Roast beef, mashed potatoes, peas and gravy are one gestalt, not four.

summer evening—
kneeling in the garden
picking tomatoes

At the end of the meal hot water is served. We wash our empty bowls and drink most of what now is a very thin broth. The small amount left is dumped into a bucket with which the kitchen staff, as their last act, waters a tree or plant.

snarling
her stout little body
rips the leaf to shreds—
strolls to her dish of water
laps it up

Not only do we, the eaters, leave no tracks (our *ōryōkis* are reassembled, tied and replaced beside our *zabutan*—there are no "dishes"), but every shred of food has been used to sustain life. Leftovers in the serving pots are rehashed into the evening's gruel. Not a scrap is wasted.

one bug
one mouth
snap!

I Dedicate this Stone

Morning ends abruptly. Noon service, preceded by the noon bell's mysterious reminder, is more amalgamated into the flesh of the day than morning or evening service. Students hastily throw on their robes over their work clothes, splash their faces with water (they always seem half washed, half sweaty) and just make it to the *zendo*.

I dedicate this stone
to the soul
of the fetus
of the mother whale
I harpooned

We open our bowls and chant. Then we eat in silence. Broken here and there by a click-click of spoon against bowl (though we try to pay attention to the way we eat so that the noise of eating does not disturb another person's concentration).

drizzly morning
a child's voice
above the surf

Somehow lunch-silence is a more surface silence than the silence at breakfast. When lunch is over (before we even leave the *zendo*) people's minds, as registered in their postures, have already moved on to something else.

after-meal lull—
sun sparkles off
an unwatched overhead screen

It is hard to stay with eating. Though strictly forbidden (during a meal one is supposed to lower one's gaze as in *zazen* and focus on the numerous aspects of meal protocol—taking the right amount of food, chewing carefully, finishing every drop, tasting the flavors, appreciating the aesthetics, feeling the appropriate gratitude and vowing to use the energy in such a way as to redeem the life of the sentient beings sacrificed on one's behalf), still one's unruly mind wanders to this and that and especially to the eating bowls of those across the aisle. How many succeed in chewing their rice, each bite fifty times, relishing the varying nuances of flavor extracted with diminishing potency as one approaches the thirties and forties? How many chew their food at all? Most of us gulp it down.

> *muddy brook*
> *broad-veined river*
> *the ocean's mouth—stuffed*

Dinner in the *zendo* is a different matter altogether. Traditionally in Buddhist monasteries monks refrain from eating after noon. Our custom of restricting the evening meal to two bowls (instead of three) is an acknowledgment of the traditional way.[2] Dinner (not a true "meal") is gruel (the day's leftovers plus a grain—the leftovers from <u>that</u> become "gruel bread") and a vegetable. The ritual is shortened, chanting eliminated. Just clappers and silent eating. Anyway, practically everyone has a stash of Oreos in his room.

hopping through the hole
too small for the starling
a bluebird peers out

---

[2] Originally, Buddhist wayfarers ate only in the early morning and at noon, and this practice continues in southern Buddhism. When the religion moved to a colder climate, a supper in the evening was added. However, out of deference to tradition, it was called the "medicine stone" and consisted only of leftovers.

SATSUKI

the moon of transplanting

Tree Frogs—Their Rubbery Croak

After *tangaryo* I'm assigned to the garden. The head gardener takes me on a guided tour of the upper and lower gardens explaining how planting, composting, weeding, and general maintenance are done. I try to grasp what she is saying, but I end up listening to her—to the quality of her presence, her probable history. I find I'm a little in love with her.

your sunny face
perched atop a six-foot stalk
along the headland's rill

Eventually she leaves. I am alone in the upper garden, which is spotless. I am squatting, digging up burdock root. While I understand that the activity of digging burdock root just now, here, is the zenith of civilized behavior, I am losing energy rapidly. My aching back, my aching knees, the mosquitoes, the boredom . . . I cannot squat another second. I bend over instead and quickly exhaust that alternative. I panic. Less than an hour has gone by.

dusk—
daylight lingers
in the suddenly-chill air

I don't make any friends. The kitchen, where I eventually end up, adheres to its own separate schedule. There are people I admire and want to get to know, but they seem inaccessible, self-contained, following a private inner, as well as outer, program.

the storm breaks—
one hermit crab
scuttles through the undertow

The Tassajara zendo kitchen is staffed with headstrong individuals: Alan, a huge person whose high-spirited presence overpowers the room; Roovane, intensely philosophical, idealistic, and principled; Donny, lithe and powerful with a deep, wild energy; and Paul, sincere but stiff and fussy about rules. I constantly have the feeling that I'm doing the wrong thing.

oncoming storm—
thunderous ghosts
patrol the horizon

There may have been a second woman, I can't recall. Wait. I do remember. It is Lucille, an older woman, an artist. Lucille and I are often told to wash lettuce. We carry towels and buckets to the porch by the creek. Lucille gabs until one of the men stares her down. As soon as they leave she yaks away as if it's the most natural thing in the world.

steamy morning
lulling me to sleep—tree frogs—
their rubbery croak

Alan, Roovane and Donny—the triumvirate. Customarily there is one *tenzo* and others do what they are told. Alan may have been *tenzo* but my predominant impression is of the three together (arguing) over trivia.

day in, day out
bull frogs and
the echo of bull frogs

The Seedling Draped in Moonlight

Kitchen work I understand. It is indoors (warm), task-oriented and private, as opposed to say cleaning guest cabins, which is indoors and task-oriented but not at all private (it is more efficient to work in teams and the guests require attention), or the garden, which is task-oriented and private but outdoors (where my hands stiffen). Other jobs, like keeper of the baths or guest-season manager, are not sufficiently labor-intensive (to contain my anxiety and make me feel cleansed).

dusk—
wincing, the old lady
swallows her medicine

The majority of the kitchen staff, now my exclusive eating partners, are rigid and somewhat puritanical macrobiotics, though they disguise these qualities (make them harder to confront) by their conviviality. My eating practices, the quantities I accept and so forth, are subject to much observation and remark. If I take a little too much salad (usually made with tomatoes and dressing—very yin), or am lax about chewing every bite of rice, the wrongness of my behavior is conveyed to me. Eating becomes petrifying. Grains are the only food about which I feel fairly safe. Grains, however, do not fill me.

spouting offshore along the bluff
gigantic hulks breach—
flukes slap the water

Also there is a time factor. The "kitchen" eats together. We chant at the time for chant, eat after the clappers indicate "begin," and wash our bowls in unison. I can't get enough.

foraging the lagoon
a hatchling
choked by weeds

I grow thinner. At first I am glad. Some months earlier I had tried to lose weight. For a brief time my energy peaks. Then the incredible heat, flies, intense schedule, and, perhaps most important for me, the lack of a kindred spirit, prevail.

brown leaves shrivel—
pock-marked fruit
fail to ripen
in the weak
October sun

I lay on my futon under the trees, under the sky, lulled to sleep by the water. I am emaciated, exhausted. I sleep a week.

washed by rain
the seedling . . .
draped in moonlight

Roovane visits me. I am finished sleeping but still too weak to move around. It's afternoon and I am hot so I unzip my sleeping bag and drag out my legs. I do feel cooler but I notice I'm wearing only underpants and a t-shirt. I make one of those mental shifts allowing myself to be exposed like this. Roovane is my brother, I tell myself. He seizes the opportunity to school me on the subject of shaving. He launches into a discourse on body hair, its naturalness and that I should allow myself to have this. It's a moral thing.

dusk—
lilies nod
in the shallow water

Suzuki-roshi is just here, joyful and simple like a boy. So long as he is present, I cannot die. At the very end of summer during our *Shosan* Ceremony, a formal ceremony during which each student presents her understanding in the form of a question, I ask, "When I awoke from my illness I saw the first red autumn leaves. Is that *zazen*?" Suzuki-roshi smiles warmly. I feel cleansed. My whole being shines.

the afternoon purrs
stroked by soft
summery light

Deer-Chewed Tips

On calendar days with a four or nine the schedule is relaxed which means fewer *zendo* activities and no work at all. The entire central portion of the day becomes personal time. I get very excited. My question (who am I?) can be addressed on a less ultimate level. Frankly, I am more interested in this less ultimate level because my efforts don't sink into such a bottomless pit.

> *fallout:*
> *I kneel*
> *to pick up the shards*

I decide to carve my own eating utensils. The metal spoon that comes with the *ōryōki* and the sterile Chinese-restaurant style chopsticks lack class (in my opinion). The chopsticks, though less inharmonious (at least they are wood), are clearly mass-produced. I want the implements of my meal practice not only to be gorgeous but carefully and thoughtfully crafted so as to honor the attention and care that go into providing me with daily sustenance.

clear blue sky
warm winds crook
the deeply yellow flower heads

I choose madrone, a soft (stunning) local wood. I sit on my doorstep and gouge out a bowl and approximate a stem that is comfortable in my hands. I go as far as I can with the gouge, then switch to a file, then sandpaper. What starts as coarse, gradually becomes smooth, each gradient of paper having its concomitant effect upon the spoon's surface. I cannot help but see the graceful shape that emerges from a stick (having been gouged, filed, sanded) as a metaphor for what is happening to me right now at this monastery.

the swamp—its musty smell—
airs in the
crisp March wind

The spoon is implicit in the tree limb. Mismanaging any part of the transformation process (drying and fumigating the wood, storing it to prevent warping, planing, sawing, filing, polishing and buffing the finished surface) can detract from its ultimate beauty. Someone might stain it and violate the nature of the madrone's inner radiance.

upside down
caked with mud . . . a tortoise's
sun-bleached bones

I relish my project. Whereas I am not able to control the weather, the schedule, the long hours of *zazen*, I can easily control these few tools.

summer afternoon—
only my pedaling
disturbs the silence

I make my chopsticks both thicker at the handle and pointier at the tip than the commercial ones. I want them to be daring (almost sexy) precision instruments. And for good reason. With the chanting and extensive ritual that surround our *zendo* meals, I can't be wasting precious minutes chasing slippery *goban* (rice). When I scoop up a bite, it needs to be a big bite so I can get on with the *suimono* (soup) and *tsukemono* (pickled vegetables) in the other two bowls.

autumn leaf
adrift in the pothole
fingers spread wide

I make the *setsu* eel-like, sleek and silky. It is light as a feather when I attach its linen tip. When hot water is poured into the Buddha bowl, the setsu is what scrapes off the grain stuck to its sides. The remaining grain-water is transferred to the second bowl where the *setsu* again is used to scrape off encrusted food. Most of this "broth" is drunk with just a small portion reserved as an offering at the meal's end. Without the *setsu* one is helpless in the face of stickiness—the very nature of food in bowls.

spring:
sprouts
from the deer-chewed tips

The Pudgy Moon

A familiar feeling comes over me on a summer afternoon in the heat, with the flies. I have already done the work I am clear about. There are other things to do, like scrubbing pots and washing floors, but I have no will. My mind goes blank. I fill the bucket with sudsy water and wring out the mop. My body feels dead. I wrench it anyway through the sweeping motions.

tamping her nest
she lumbers away—
laden with dirt

Harriet is here. With her delicate body, waist-long flaming red hair, and the strident immaculateness of her maintenance of these assets, it is as if she bloomed here, full-grown, without a history.

broad-winged bird
silhouette swaying
in the noontide

Harriet is sweet and amazingly successful at achieving Japanese standards of beauty. Her smallness permits her to be elaborate in a simple way. Tiny movements, sexy hair, little black flats—very prim yet eager. Harriet has real taste. Pulsating taste.

teeny flowers—
their fragrance
in a shallow breeze

I like Harriet and do not turn down her friendship. Intimate talk—a relic from the outside world—is normalizing. We go to the baths and pour over her romance. I immerse myself in the specifics, grateful for the reprieve. Her tales sparkle with fire. My own mediocrity and lack of strength evaporate for a moment.

chestnut wings
warming them
in the morning sun

Donny is attracted to me. I guess this though I feel awkward in his presence, as if all that I know from my life thus far has no place in his "belief system" (he would deny he has one). Therefore I am the one to be taught—he the teacher. He notices I shave my legs. Wrong. What do I do that for? I know nothing about macrobiotics, not just the food but the essential place on the scale of yin-yang of every single aspect of life. I know nothing about Zen or yoga or sex. My ignorance is astounding though I do know (unconsciously) that the teaching I can receive must be presented via softer media. His judgments sting, couched as they are within a forceful pursuing of me.

winging low
    over a field
        whose
            springtime
                bluets
                    are
                      gone

On our hike he is leading. He skips across the stream catlike from stone to stone. I loiter on the bank paralyzed to make a move, noticing that the rocks are slippery and too far apart for me.

toppled bulrush:
lingering in its stalks
the pudgy moon

MINA-ZUKI

the waterless moon

My Box-Shaped Room

After a summer at Tassajara I become a resident at the Berkeley Zen Center. My box-shaped room with high walls lined in burlap has a tall narrow window, hard wood floors, and my harpsichord. Gazing out at an exquisite monkey tree, I feel contained but very unhappy.

dusk—
creeping fog
darkens the estuary

The *zendo* itself is in the attic. Two other students live below, like me, in single rooms. Mine is the middle. Adjacent to our rooms is a living room, dining room, and kitchen. It is a big old house with a huge rambling yard.

high noon:
a Persian yawns
sprawls across the stoop

I eat almost nothing. After *zazen* in the morning (it is still dark) I walk up to the University of California cafeteria and have tea. I put many lemons in my tea and eat the lemons but that's all. I have more tea at noon, and at night I try not to eat dinner. I stay in my room instead, drinking something warm, sucking something suckable.

no-necked crane
plumage folded
one
leg
lifted
off
the
sandbar

Other people are having dinner in the dining room just outside my door, but I refuse. When I do eat, I need to be alone. People and noise disturb me. Of course I am starving. Around midnight, when everyone is asleep, I go to the refrigerator and scavenge through leftovers. Or else I stand in the pantry and dip raisins in peanut butter, eating them compulsively for a long time.

> *o caterpillar . . .*
>   *in your wake*
>   *a sump of leaves*

Hoisting His Wings Toward the Trespasser

I have life in fleeting moments: the clarity of the pre-dawn *zendo*, soft, fragrant, alive; the initial sounds of becoming still infusing itself into my tired body; later the birds and a sense of place, here, for a moment; the terror of my scale, pulling it from the closet in my still-dark room, making out the numbers; catching a glimpse of the nubile monkey tree enframed by my curtainless window; having tea at school just as the cafeteria opens—sitting here entitled to sit for this brief time. After that my body hurts. By 7:00 a.m. I am beat.

one Monarch
nomad in these hills—
even the sun
rises later and later in the chilly sky

I can't get comfortable. (My harpsichord stool is not.) I am never warm. I am never full. I have no friends and I can't read (a curious side-effect of Zen practice).

fallout . . .
a radio blares
through the empty hallway

One day around 4:00 p.m. I go to my room, lie on the floor, and stare at the ceiling. My life has never felt so wrong. I question my decision to study music, which is turning out to be too technical and too physically taxing. My room is not a haven because there is no place for me. Accommodating me requires a disruption. I am already fully disrupted. The slightest further disruption is unbearable to me. I want my room to remain in perfect aesthetic balance while I drift in and out ghostlike, tracklessly. I cannot tolerate evidence of my own existence.

a full-throated call—
arching, hoisting his wings
toward the trespasser

I mentally review the people in my life, mostly Zen people as I have (predictably) met no-one in the music department. I sort of care for the Zen people. Since they are trying to do what I am trying to do, we have something in common I tell myself. But am I trying to do what they are trying to do? Why don't I *feel* the common bond? The truth is I don't feel care for a single soul.

cross-legged I sit
with my back toward these
annoying birds

It is 2:00 a.m. Everyone is asleep but the floors creak and sound carries throughout the house. I know this but ignore it. I am alone with the moon in the dining room. For a moment I have me but in a contorted, embryonic way. My body and will are exhausted. Kneeling by the refrigerator mauling through food only to exhaust this too, I despise myself, punish myself, until several nights later the same convoluted geeklike energy rises again, turns inward on itself—feeding off itself—this cycle is my life. It is disgusting and serves no one, but it is all I have.

slouching toward the toilet
night wind sears me
to the bone

Teeny Sprouts Everywhere

I am astonished to be told I can begin sewing a *rakusu*. Suzuki-roshi will give me a Buddhist name and write it alongside his on the back. It means I have a lineage, that my existence falls into a context—those following the Way of my teacher and his ancestors, dating back presumably to Dogen Zenji.

slickened by rain
slabs of mud
glisten in the after-sun

I feel placed. No longer arbitrary, my actions are now informed by codes of conduct that over the centuries enlightened beings have found to be helpful in carrying one beyond ignorance. In Buddhism I find not only an understanding of my suffering but a remedy for it. The fact that I already am showing signs of being a misfit endears the privilege to me all the more since it proves its inclusivity, thus, I think, its profundity.

hovering around the bloodroot—
fresh billmark
across its wing

Issan's decision not to ask Suzuki-roshi for ordination, and instead just to do the best he can, would never satisfy me. Here is what is important to me as I prepare myself formally to become Suzuki-roshi's disciple:

Sitting at the end of a large oak table, in a corner near a window, relishing the pristine winter afternoon sun as it spreads warmth and light on our assortment of sewing utensils.
Feeling a sense of belonging because I have been included, yet suspecting that if they knew my real nature, they wouldn't have.
The solidity of the needle as I guide it through its painstaking procedure and the pliant cotton thread, the integrity of this.
Avoiding the mantra we are supposed to chant inwardly at each stitch, excusing myself from this part of it, assuring myself it is not important.
The passing of time. Sewing binds my anxiety, holds me steady.

The chair, the table, the light, the process of making stitches, and the frustration of being delayed when I need help, having to wait for the instructor to finish helping others. I know I want to be doing this, but I never seriously consider what "this" is, what it means (to allow—nay, assist others to precede me), am I qualified, can I really live the life of a bodisattva?

moonlit path . . .
step by step
to pee

San Rei Ei Sho. Katagiri-sensei translates for me: "Great Mountain Eternal Supreme Enlightenment." He says the *Ei* is special because it is the same *Ei* as in *Eiheiji*, the renowned Japanese Zen Temple.

the sun sets—
a migrant's pale shadow
over the sea

I like my name immediately. It feels whole, sonorous, larger than me. I am slightly disappointed when Katagiri-sensei renders it into English. I think, "It's so vague. What does it mean—'great mountain'—and everybody eventually achieves 'eternal supreme enlightenment:'" I can't relate to it.

swollen streambed:
depositing her egg
on its cavernous bank

Others get names with tangibility and (more importantly) guidance. Mine seems too grand. I may get to something important eventually but I do it by rote effort, focusing on banal details. My fortitude more accurately resembles that of a rocking chair.

mud-washed hill:
teeny sprouts
everywhere

Deaf to the Whistling Winter Birds

Unfortunately the sewing of my *rakusu* (my relationship with sewing it) is bound up with my relationship with the Berkeley Zen Center. Situated in the flats, an old part of town with sprawling, dilapidated, though still picturesque homes, the Berkeley Zen Center—with its old old trees, flower garden, and immense backyard—offers itself up as a world.

> *a puff of cloud . . .*
>   *its trailing edge*
>   *in the quiescent sky*

One clanks through its rooms whose shabby elegance is on the one hand compelling and on the other disappointing. It looks congenial. Windows and floors gleaming from morning *soji*—it looks as if one could easily do anything here, never having to worry about spilling something or damaging something. But for me the general excludes the specific. "Anything" adds up to anything except my thing, which might be for example to read undisturbed in a well-supported chair with lots of light and footstool for any two hours that suit me.

*April thaw—
twigs in ice
cover the bud*

A second factor contributes to my "displaced" personhood. Strive though he does to manifest the qualities Issan displays naturally, Mel, in his early fifties, falls short of the requisite understanding. Though he might be the first to admit this, even in the admission there is a falling short. Behind his "humility" lay an enormous pride that expresses itself in the predictability of his choices, for example, always for the lesser, the more common—which is a rigidity in itself—a staunch personal preference fronted as a whim that loses legitimacy on repetition.

with whiplash speed
plowing through the swamp
lily pads stuck to his dome

Underneath what isn't really ease (and that is the problem) is a tenacity more than matched by my own pitifully misguided tenacity. The more desperate we are, the more powerfully we hold on to our defenses. I am more desperate, therefore more tenacious and Mel isn't prepared for this. He lacks the training.

rain—
a bird perches
on the railing
talons clinging to the
freshly painted bar

What unfolds is not exactly a battle of wills. I am trying in my own way to be flexible and do what the situation requires. He, having accepted me into the household, is also trying, but is feeling undoubtedly intense disappointment, anger, frustration, and helplessness. I am not what he expected nor what the community needs.

roiling, tumbling,
riding the winter wind—
witch grass

I am in a false position. My scale, my room with no place to be, the music department to which I am likewise unsuited, my lack of friends or ability to have friends, my temperament, which is incompatible not only to Zen practice but to communal practice of any kind, and my body, whose needs overrun the stringent schedule (anorexia, while confining me to a physical/emotional straightjacket, is actually a dysfunctional attempt to address them) add up to an entirely untenable situation.

dry red leaves
plowing through them
on my tricycle

Mel, as practice leader, needs to come to me and talk frankly about how and why I am not working out. He tries once. Once morning he suggests we go out for breakfast and attempts to reason with me. But it is too late. The cold war leading up to this "breakfast" has hardened my heart against him. The very fact that we are at "King Pin Donuts" shows he doesn't understand.

necks cross
puffs condense
in the icy air

Much earlier he could have 1) asked me to leave 2) made the issues open ones so that at least we discussed them regularly, and/or 3) changed the expectations around the responsibilities of the *zendo* residents. For my part, I feel that I am a lot more in attendance than the other resident who does almost nothing, though he is available socially. I am not available socially but I cook, clean, garden, and minister in the *zendo*. My efforts go unacknowledged because something else is the matter. Mel freezes. I already serve an icy master. Warmth might have melted me, but ice simply stiffens my upper lip, the better to contend with my adversary of choice.

under ice, under mud
deaf to the whistling
winter birds

BOOK THREE
Rivers

NAGA-TSUKI
the moon of the heads of rice

Like the Wild Dogs Who Yelp and Snap Defending
a Random Street Corner

I awaken to a certain kind of quiet that only occurs in the early morning. No one stirs. I feel that the world—all parts of it that I need and nothing extra—is utterly available to me.

shhh . . .

   listen . . .

      the swale is thawing

I arrange a kettle of water to boil while I wash and put on something warm. Then I make the best coffee I know how, hand-grinding the beans and so forth. When it is done I turn off the light and take my coffee into a large bare room. I can see above and into the quiet streets.

sunrise—
swelling in the marsh water
new grass

It is this particular minute to which I feel I belong. I know definitely that I am alive. And I know that I have to work hard (strain psychically) to stay alive. I listen intently to the silence, to the lack of anything stirring but the slight creak of my rocker against the hardwood floor.

the city sleeps
an old man's rod
dangles in the surf

Next door lives an older couple. It is still dark as I walk by and I can easily see the man as he paddles around his kitchen. He wears workman's clothing and I picture him filling his lunchbox while his water boils for tea.

sleeping willow:
aroused by the morning's
low-lying breeze

In the dark, in the cold, panicked to face two packs of wild dogs who regularly roam the neighborhood at this hour I think, "Here he is all safe in a situation that's both predictable and fulfilling. He obviously takes pleasure in his morning routine. He knows what he's going to do, that he can do what he's going to do, and how what he does fits into the larger scheme of his life. He fits into his life."

spinning orange and yellow
through the sunny pool . . .
little cooter, your spots

This in contrast to me who feels stranded—in my self, in my day, in my existence—that even now I am in a vulnerable position, if not a virtually dangerous one. I am a stray, like the wild dogs who yelp and snap defending a random street corner, all they have in the way of territory.

northbound monarch
hugging the coast
in the after-storm

Even as You Screech Your Imminent Silence

The air is crisp—not cold and sunny à la sparkling winter mornings, but cool with a soft clean light. A bank of clouds clings to the horizon.

sea birds dodge
the white foamed waves—
at sunset their soft chittering

I have the impulse to pare down my life, to examine it more closely, tighten it up—a familiar desire that rears its head at unpredictable intervals and insists on being addressed. Typically my wardrobe comes under attack. My ongoing dilemma—what is mine and not mine, what is right and not right when it comes to clothing and adornments of my body—has never been resolved.

surveying his juniper snag
a bluebird stills . . .
the flycatcher flees

It is very important to me to feel that my clothing is authentic, thoughtfully constructed, and functional without getting in the way of me. Wendy, for example, has wonderful clothes and wears them thoroughly, cleaning and cooking in them all day long—"As clothes are intended," I think, "not like I use them in snippets, for tiny portions of my life, as if they require preserving."

even as you screech
your imminent
silence

I determine to have only one thing to wear. It must be hand-made and designed by me—which turns out to be "fat pants" and an Indian style over-blouse. I sew this ensemble in three different fabrics: a blue-white feather-weight cotton, an adobe-colored double-layered gauze, and a copper velour, warm and cuddly. The three versions provide flexibility and depth. They need very few accessories. A part of me feels I have hit upon the solution, solved my clothing-koan once and for all. Which is what I want—a final me.

balanced on a sunflower
her wings—encased in his—
grow quiet

Due to constant vacillations, my closet is a hodgepodge of bits of me. I want a consistent me, a me I can know beforehand and rely upon. I want to be able to say (the thought of such a self-contained statement is of enormous comfort) "I limit my clothing to 'fat pants, sweaters, and soft cotton t-shirts." No sooner are the words uttered then I purchase some gorgeous ethnic blouse with richly embroidered sacred designs.

beside the impatiens
feathering the air
first one, then five . . .

Spearing the Sun as it Sets on the Pylons

Sometimes I will see something, buy it on a whim and then go home and get rid of everything that lacks the vision of this thing.

autumn . . .
on a barely-detectable
north wind

I never shop with an agenda. I have a few extra hours, find myself near a store and take it from there.

hot summer day:
jinking about the hummocks of sand
red-eyed flies

Take the nightgown I bought for example. It is white Indian gauze, a sort of handkerchief cotton, and absolutely plain. It is full length and without sleeves, so simple it frightens me.

autumn:
petals cover
the sparrow's body

The white rayon dress is also Indian. It has short-sleeves, a V-neck and a tunic that falls three-quarters of the way down over a skirt of the same material. The tunic opens in the front and drapes gracefully from a bodice. Its plainness makes my ears ring.

spring morning—
a speckled egg
on the grassy hummock

My splurges are consistent, apparel of some sort or containers—boxes, folders, tin cans. A flame kindles inside me when I recognize an item as mine. Always it enlightens—clarifies, articulates, points in a direction hitherto only implied. My purchases inevitably make sense as acts of aesthetic maturation.

from treelimb to violet
little imago's
almost-somersault

Recently I noticed someone in the *zendo* wearing red. I question whether it is appropriate for a Buddhist to call attention to herself in this way. (I don't stop to distinguish between codes of dress for the *zendo* versus codes for daily life.) Suddenly I am aware of how loud the color red is, how it attracts (demands) attention, how I, by taking red for one of "my" colors, must have unconsciously been demanding attention all my life.

scarlet wings
    in the brewing storm
        scuttle by the lake

My eyes pop open. Yes. I am sure of it. As a prospective priest, I can't be going around giving off signals to pay attention to me. I rip through my closet, my drawers, my shelves. Everything red is removed. Which feels clean, uncluttered, as if at last, I have achieved a correct understanding.

monarch:
spearing the sun as it sets
on the pylons

HA-ZUKI

the moon in which the leaves fall

Two Fat Dove-Colored Birds Waddling their Way along a Eucalyptus Branch

I decide to move to The San Francisco Zen Center. It is the only viable option.

skiff of snow:
on the barbed wire
a pupa blows

The rightness of which is seemingly confirmed this first Saturday morning. Arriving early I am in plenty of time for lecture. Unfamiliar with the protocol, I stand in back alongside visitors who prefer chairs. I look directly at Baker-roshi. He looks directly at me, intently, discovering me. In a flash I feel seen. He "gets" who I am in a matter of seconds.

air
clear
cool
the
through
calls
warbler
a
May flowers:

My scholarship at Zen Center includes my room, which I love, all my basic food expenses, and a $50-per-month stipend. I don't understand money. I almost resent my mother's periodic gifts because I will just be getting in touch with how much I have (so I feel nestled in my little amount) when another arbitrary sum arrives and plummets me into confusion. My father, on the other hand, is so stingy that I simultaneously pity him and am furious that he can so forthrightly ignore my needs.

your silver girth
rips the sea—
sea wrack tossed
sea stock rocking
in the tumbling pebbles

I feel secure in my tiny room. The closet holds a few clothes and the built-in chest a few belongings. Just as there is little chance for excess (lack of restraint) in the haiku I allow myself to write, this circumscribed space provides a measure of safety.

shells along the sill
a shallow breeze
crosses my desk

Puttering around I look up and see two fat dove-colored birds waddling their way along a Eucalyptus branch. Their movements show exquisite attunement. I am spellbound. "I wonder what kind of birds those are?" I think, not caring in the slightest.

sunrise:
snowflakes dust
the new-born chick

Spitting Out the Queen

Dokusan until now has been with Suzuki-roshi who restricts questions to *zazen* practice. I am not sure what to expect from this American man who certainly would be capable of adding a more intimate dimension to the private student-teacher relationship. I guess I actually expect he wants to talk about my becoming *anja* since this is a job he recently has asked me to do. I do my bows and sit down. Baker-roshi instantly inquires, "Why are you so thin?" So right away we don't see eye to eye.

my bead of sweat
cooling you
this sweltering night

While I am piercingly thin, it is as though no one can see—the visible part of me being so unrelated to piercingly-thin me. The thinness comes from an inner imperative, exerting enough control so that I can feel substantial (as opposed to vacuous) and can experience existence through my sense of will.

iridescent checker
your prenatal profile
etched evermore deeply . . . darkly . . .

Under Baker-roshi *dokusan* is a lot like psychotherapy with these differences:
1) one waits for an indefinite period of time beforehand
2) the session begins with a series of three full prostrations and other bowing
3) the teacher can end the session at any point by ringing a bell and
4) there's no telling when one will be able to come back.

alders
the
above
curly- *cry*
cues *your*
of *tailing*
mist

With Suzuki-roshi such procedures make sense. He is a compassionate master. One welcomes the opportunity to be corrected by him, to acknowledge one's respect and gratitude. Baker-roshi's including personal matters (feelings, relationships, major and minor life-decisions) without the support of regularity, consistency, and count-on-able meetings, brings one to a no-man's land. People's lives are on hold for months because he is inexplicably unavailable.

outside the tube
an old rose-peddlar's
empty stall

One Saturday afternoon I am scheduled to have *dokusan* with Baker-roshi. I know he will be late. I think, "Why should I wait? I don't want to wait." So I go next door to clean his house, which is part of my job as *anja*. As I clean I think, "It's silly to have so many knickknacks. They are useless and collect dust." Unobservant of my disrespectful (and, indeed, ungrateful) state of mind I proceed, "Maybe it's his wife's doing. Virginia is an obnoxious woman always rushing around full of herself. She isn't even a Zen student." It dawns on me as curious that most of the senior men at Zen Center happen to be with women who don't sit zazen. Baker-roshi doesn't sit very much zazen. Still I think, as I speculate if I dare squeeze in his laundry too, "He is the one who should be doing this. He needs to wash his own socks."

spitting out the Queen
the yellow bird's
shrill call

Arrested by a Flower in the Verdant Gulch

An old shriveled Japanese nun who sews like lightning comes to Zen Center. Sewing is her practice. The swiftness, deftness, and sheer energy that she brings to this work, sitting in *seiza*, perfectly comfortable, is contagious to those who join her. I get very excited. Sewing (silent, intense, thrifty) is something I can do, especially Japanese sewing (magnificently intelligent yet at the same time mindless, so that it becomes a body practice, one with delicacy and subtlety).

after the chase
arrested by a flower
in the verdant gulch

She herself is sewing a robe for Baker-roshi. Soon I notice that most of the students in the room also are sewing robes. It takes me awhile to realize that they are sewing their own priest's robes, that they are going to be ordained and that this nun has been invited here expressly to help them do this.

splashing wet leaves
in the cool moist air
a male hummer flits
to the hophornbeam's
topmost branches

I am surprised because the students are (some of them) quite new and I never dreamed they would so quickly attain the permission conscientiously (now it does seem very calculated) withheld from me. Then it dawns on me, "I am in this room with the pressing question, 'Can sewing become my life's work?'" I take for granted being a nun and the issue is about what "specialty" I will have in this "field." I study her person, her stamina, her shiny eyes to see if I can measure up—if my life can in any way simulate her life. Others are just here. They aren't making any big decisions.

the city sleeps
one black duck
surfs the shallow tide

FUMI-ZUKI
the moon in which the nights grow long

Chewing, Excreting . . . Whorls of Leaves

In the context of a monastery where the custom is not to distinguish oneself—to meld as seamlessly as possible into the daily routine—my solo stunt (I am passionate about my thinness . . . I am on fire for this practice of staying very thin) burns like a cut on the community's finger. For me it is be thin or die.

groping, missing—
a black-masked hunter
rakes the twilight

During low periods I binge, which brings me much lower. Binges are virulent and have their own life span, their own arising and falling. One will click on and I am utterly at its mercy. Efforts to control it are fruitless and take away the pleasure of mindlessly eating for hours and hours. It has to be mindless and it has to be "endless," otherwise it doesn't satisfy. Part of the joy is abandoning one's consciousness and entering a sphere where one is uncondemned.

noisy city
the old woman
lost in her peach

There is also the iniquity, the barbaric and primitive grasping with which one is shameless before the urge to fill one's mouth. And it is the mouth, not stomach, that is the highlighted region. Quantities of food are washed through the mouth—often food which in a different frame of mind would be unpalatable, crude, or disgusting.

the old bowl
filled with snow
first he slurps
then knocks it over
as he slouches away

Once in motion, the progression of a binge is absolutely regular. I eat mountains of whatever tipped it off. This is invariably followed by anything I can lay my hands on, first that is rich (with butter or cheese), second that is starchy, and lastly that is sweet. A typical finale might be a box of filled chocolates. Curiously, these stages are irreversible. It seems as if it would hardly matter, but by the time I have entered stage three, for example, foods from the previous stages are unappealing.

nibbling the blade
    chewing, excreting...
        whorls of leaves

Afterwards I sleep. I sleep as if passed out, sometimes till late in the afternoon of the following day.

sunset:
a mower recedes
to the other side of the hillock

Waking from a binge one feels sluggish, toxic, putrid. I want to sleep more, drown out the rest of my life too. That day I rarely eat anything. By the next I am fairly stable, though ashamed, humiliated, and aware that it is not over. It will happen again. Nay—I will see to it—look forward to and prepare for it again. The mere thought of it makes me tingle with excitement.

a monarch pupa cracks—
tiny ichneumon wasps
scramble into sunlight

Hey You—

My face wears a mask whose rouged cheeks and cherry lips shine through a light coat of powder. A tortoise-shell comb probes the tips of my coffiure. Though I have on geta and carry some sort of lantern, my iridescent face—not the white of a face drained of color, but the white of transparency . . . the color of no color—peers from a hollow hole.

midnight:
in one haywire jolt
the forest's silhouette

I take many showers. I desperately need to shower. I feel I will go berserk if my shower is taken away.

delicate crescent:
bathed by the light
of a half moon

One day I am in the produce section of the Greengrocer, Zen Center's neighborhood store, when Pam Chernoff comes up to me and accuses me of stealing lemons. I do steal them. I steal food not only from the Greengrocer but from the store down the street, Safeway, and any other grocery I happen to be in (as, by the way, do many anorexic and bulemic women). I know I steal food and that I have stolen food for years, but I have repeated my justification so often to myself that I feel entitled to what I take. Stealing is slightly exciting and very practical. I don't stop to consider that taking what has not been given is contradictory to the very precepts by which I represent myself as living—that it is impossible to be in a boat and go in opposite directions at the same time.

stuffing creamers in her bag
turning, leaving—
the woman's eyes

To be confronted about stealing is equivalent to being confronted with anorexia. "No! No! No!" I lie through my teeth. It is a lame lie, transparent, whatever pops out of my mouth. Pam knows I am lying. I sort of know I am lying (I need to lie so badly I don't entirely "know"). I make myself not think about Pam's knowing. I deny it with some dopey explanation which, to her credit, she accepts. No doubt the staff had a meeting about this problem. Pam was asked to talk to me and all were aware that no matter how ardently I denied the accusation (which I'm sure they predicted I would do), the confrontation would nevertheless serve its purpose of probably stopping me (helping me). It may have done that. It is certainly one of the more beneficial-to-me behind-the-scenes conversations that affect me deeply but in which I am not included.

> *hey you—*
> *perched*
> *at my back door*
> *filling your beak*
> *with water*

The Simple Act of Toast-Eating

When I am given the job of baker my heart opens to these Zen people. Because I take it to mean that they understand me. They see that I can't do what others are able to do, so they give me something else that has its own internal imperatives.

beggar's bag around my neck
bundle over shoulder—
hey, that's Saigyō's shadow

There is a moment in the morning, after breakfast is over, the large platters and steam trays having been put away, and before a crew arrives for lunch preparation, when I am in the kitchen alone. My loaves are in the oven. Soon I can take a nap. In the afternoon I will package and deliver my bread in Zen Center's van. At this particular juncture I have just about completed a good day's output and feel myself as available (to the universe) as I ever feel in my life.

white bird, blue sky
wingspan arched
gilded by the sunlight

This would be about 9:30 a.m. Suddenly into my world enters young Rusa, the Chinese-American girlfriend of one of our senior students. She is utterly lovely—thin, trim, composed. Not being a Zen student herself, she does not abide by our daily schedule. In fact it looks as though she is just getting up and coming into the kitchen (as an ordinary person would) to make herself some toast, which she proceeds to do, sitting at a little table eating it, reading the paper (as an ordinary person would).

passing a cow
    four cranes . . . graze
        the summer pasture

I am dumbfounded. Every feature of her—her beauty, her composure, her relationship, her privileges, her routine, her having her own life—here condensed into the simple act of toast-eating—flaunts itself at the core of my being. "How can she!" I shout mentally, which means "How can she know herself well enough to have made the choices that give her such freedom?"

wedged in the pocket
of the drowned boy—
blossoms of butterbur

I feel intensely alone. I continually get from others the impression that everything else (anything else) is more important than me. I exist as an object, appearing where I am supposed to, doing what I am supposed to, just like in my childhood home. Which is to say I am not seen, but wanting this is now out-of-step with the entire Buddha Dharma.

gliding
shuddering
wing-tip stunned
by the
wire

BOOK FOUR *Sky*

KAMINA-ZUKI
the godless moon

Stinging Nettle Leaf

It is luxurious to sleep past 4:00 a.m. (Danny is back in my life and has invited me to visit him in Chicago.) I wash in his bathroom and putter around. The day is mine.

my cat yawns
its slender throat
gulps the pale sun

I arrange my writing tools on a large flat surface. It feels right to be in an unpretentious apartment working (my work) while Danny is somewhere doing his work, making the money to support this. (I can pretend for a minute.)

stinging nettle leaf . . .
glued underneath
her small pile of eggs

I imagine myself going on and on, elevated overnight (by virtue of Danny) to a place where I can write and have the activity of my writing taken seriously. Like today, I think, I'll write for most of the morning. Then I'll take a walk, clean the house, bake, all things I'm good at.

she cocks her head—
algae wave
in the sunny floodwater

Once the phone rings. It is Danny to see how I am. Irrationally (because he is being very considerate and of course has no idea I am writing/ "working") I feel slighted, as if somehow my work is interruptible, not warranting the vacuum-packed environment I insist upon and feel deprived without.

    poof . . .
      your lacy path
        over the vast
      mountainface
   rockslide

Out in a T-Shirt

Light sparkles through the cold air illuminating in a nostalgic way a certain parochial quality to the concrete sidewalk with its grassy crevices. A Lucky's seems futuristic. Old Jewish ladies lug their groceries, head scarves tied beneath their chin.

the breath of almost-rain
on the tree-lined streets . . .
out in a t-shirt

I decide to make bread and surprise Danny with six fresh loaves. I buy everything I need, carry it back and work on my bread the whole afternoon. While the bread bakes I sit *zazen*, improvising a *zafu*. There is no context (I can tell) for *zazen* in this house. I sit anyway, wanting to finally, feeling it is the right thing to do despite the lack of the room's resonance.

hunt over . . .
    a water lily
        bobs in the waves

Slowly it emerges—all my day's activities are foreign here: writing the way I write (intensely but not scholarly), taking an aimless walk, baking as a professional bakes (in sizable batches), and sitting *zazen* methodically. His house (his life) is not set up for this. I can do my things, but I sense I'd be better off if I keep them invisible.

dead stalks of kitayoshi
conceal the nest
from the gunman

Cakes Rising on the Stove

I am full (emotionally and spiritually) by the time Danny comes home. The house (I notice) reverberates with the aroma from the bread and the vibrations from my meditation. Danny doesn't notice.

dusk
      cakes rising on the stove . . .
           the moon

He fixes himself a martini and sits down in the living room to focus on consuming it along with salted nuts. I get the impression that this is a routine. Instinctively I sit on the floor next to him.

starless sky
nosing the flask-shaped chamber—
five flashes of white

I want to hear about (so I can picture) him having breakfast, working in his lab and examining patients. "Where did you eat breakfast?" I begin my barrage of questions. Begrudgingly (with a slight tinge of indulging me) he explains that he either forgets to eat breakfast or sometimes he hears the horn of a vendor and buys donuts. That happened today. He didn't eat lunch. He seems irritable and asks me not to sit on the floor.

slapping them, grabbing them,
swiping them
out of my hair

The martini is having its effect. He begins talking and tells me the story of today's leukemia patient who is in remission and explains the ultimately irreversible degenerative process involved in having a serious blood disease. He can only help so much. Eventually the person will die.

two Siamese
tails erect—
stare at the injured bird

He fixes a second martini and we talk more about his helplessness to help the few people he does see, the frustrations with his laboratory experiments and problems in general with being on the staff of the University of Chicago Medical School. He'd like to move he says in a tone that implies it will never happen.

sun-dried cattle tracks—
flapping its wings
a hawk departs

Painted Lady in the Understory's Half-Light

Years ago Danny visited me in St. Louis and we went on a boat ride. I had on bermuda shorts and one of my father's floppy white shirts. Danny was rowing when something happened and the boat tipped over. We landed in the water and had to swim out, which we both easily could do.

shroud of fog
mallards bob
among the spongy islands

I was amused to see Danny mess up. Danny was mortified, not that he'd made a rowing mistake, but at how my mother would construe his intentions when he, who was responsible for me, brought me home dripping wet in my now transparent clothing.

gust of wind—
a hairstreak tips
on its maple leaf perch

His fears (preoccupations?) were so far from how I knew my mother, who deeply respected Danny, would feel that they gave me insight into what was gradually emerging as his guilt-ridden (Catholic?) psyche. Here again was his old newspaper-reporter consciousness: "Young Man Attempts Seduction: Lake Exploits," whereas I just thought, "Where's the seduction? Let's have more of that!"

tippling with dew
painted lady
in the understory's half-light

Caught By the Fiery Sun

Another time I visited Danny at Johns Hopkins. I read. I had fantasies and spent my time mentally preparing for the part orchestrated by my latest one.

zigzagging up
gliding down
teeny alpine

Uncertain of the situation, I had brought with me a negligee. Once I spent the whole morning arranging myself in it so that when Danny arrived, it would look (very casual) like I, in my intense business, hadn't had time to change. I had no concentration for anything except holding myself ready for the moment of his entrance.

night falls—
lying on a bed of leaves
the moon

When Danny finally arrived, clearly preoccupied with the events of his full morning, he seemed startled and a little miffed at what now seems my ridiculous (and contrived) appearance. He only stayed a moment. I was humiliated by my pretense, the dishonesty that lead to it, the lack of self-knowledge that leads to dishonesty, the fear behind that, and the instability and lack of centeredness at the bottom. As I closed the door behind him I caught a glimpse of myself in the mirror. I looked pathetic—desperate, overly-dressed, made-up (to be something I'm not—probably sexy) and totally inappropriate. Blue jeans and a sweatshirt might have been right.

little snout
beyond the jetty
flanked by flowers

I talk to Carol who is at Radcliffe and suddenly we are scheming. Why doesn't she come to visit too! It doesn't occur to me to wonder why I am so in need of Carol's lifeline in this precious circumstance of being Danny's medical school guest. I simply respond to the exciting idea that Carol might come.

horse-mint ripe . . .
a din of silverspots
in the noontime hush

Carol is her bubbly witty self and Danny is crazy about her. This is good to a point but I noticed that something in Danny that had been inactive around me was now active. There was a charge to the energy that he directed her way, as discretely as possible, but I noticed. I couldn't help but notice. It was in my face every time they spoke, which made me wonder if she was aware of it or possibly even encouraging it.

spring-green leaf tips erase the sky

At dinner one evening in the student cafeteria I got the feeling that if I weren't there it would have been an improvement. Sitting there (as I unavoidably was) watching as they spoke to each other across the formica table, I felt diminished in my being, erased from the world of ordinary people. It was almost as if (as in the bar scene with Clare in Woody Allen's *Another Woman*) the lights dimmed around my recessed figure, simultaneously brightening and warming on the pair as their conversation gripped them in an unexpected yet all the more refreshing bond of recognition and respect.

behind the shrubs
at the field's verge
caught by the fiery sun

An Orange-Black Heap Against the Gaslit Curb

Yet another time, Danny unexpectedly came to visit me at Northwestern. He was visibly uncomfortable in my grandmotherly space with its white chenille spreads and old lace curtains. The only place to sit was on the bed. In one look, which said "There's nothing for me here," he conveyed that removing his overcoat was hardly worth the trouble.

moonless night—
the edges of my cot
absorb the rain

He hailed a taxi which swept us to a restaurant, the sort of place one's first thought is "Am I dressed okay?" Like his letters, his conversation imbued the banal with the universal, the indigenous with the ethnographic. I had to strain to keep up.

big blue butterfly
        past my eyes and
      out
          to
              sea

After dinner he invited me to his hotel room. I was ablaze. We lay down on his bed and he held me for a long time. He began removing my clothing, my blouse, my slip. I was prepared to dedicate my life to him. Being here with him, enveloped in the sense of somehow this being a beginning for endless passionate times, lifted me to another level of consciousness. Sexually we had never gone this far and I was very excited.

rising wind—
a wild iris
totters from the clifftop

Suddenly (suddenly) the old familiar words entered my ears, "I have to get you home." I stiffened to contain my tears and barely managed to on the ride back. I couldn't talk. I couldn't say goodbye. Danny said goodbye when the taxi let me off. I didn't hear from him for a long time.

ghostly wings—
an orange-black heap
against the gaslit curb

SHIMO-TSUJI
the hoar-frost moon

Re-Entering the Mountain

It rains. Gusts of wind wisp through the shrubs and trees outside my door sounding elusive, threatening. It rains all night and into the morning so that I awake to the rhythmical sound of dripping from the low-hanging eaves. The steady beat is hypnotizing and for a few minutes I drop back to sleep. I feel deliciously comfortable, my body suspended. A sense of warmth oozes over my chest.

listening, dozing . . .
as it taps
my window pane

Rain warms the mountain air and feels soothing as it softly falls through the moonlight. Shallow drafts brush my face. Whereas minutes ago I felt reluctant, tired, mean, suddenly I am overcome with gratitude. In the *zendo* I sit bolt upright, supported by the gurgling creek. A chorus of birds are so ardently chirping that there seems to be a wall of raspy but sweet wet life surrounding me on all sides.

drizzly day . . .
darts and wiggles
in the waterweed

Bop. Bop. Bop. Like a woodpecker only gigantic, the *han* echoes its third round. The roshi's feet are scuffing behind me as I face the wall. He is barefoot, of course, but being large, his feet drag along the zendo's clean narrow aisle and sound like my father's house-slippers. The electricity of his presence pierces my shallow zazen.

moonlight . . .
deep in the bracts
of a pink wildflower

Morning *zazen* ends. We leave our cushions and the primordial quiet that sinks in with the raindrops. The steady pound of rain, its persistent motion, makes our straight-backed cross-legged posture seem all the more still. By the end of second period we are nestled here forever.

a train whistle blows . . .
perched in a tree
crow closes its eyes

Sutrās (literally "warp" of the dharma) are sermons of the Buddha. Robes draped gracefully, legs tucked under forming a base to our statuesque torsos, we momentarily embody these syllables, each of which, honored by its own thump of the *mokugyō*, hammers into our being again and again and again. They are startling, even without the translation.

morning glories
stumbling upon them
outside my gate

Rain Bends the Umbel

A warm glow from kerosene lamps beckons through the vaporous light. Cackles from the fire and scrapings of chair-legs are foreground sounds. Sacred texts wrapped in cloth rest in front of each person. Clack-clack go the clappers and each enters her own carefully selected realm of the Buddhist universe.

rain
bends the umbel . . .
the fritillary below

Suzuki-roshi doesn't press scholarship. He says since we have one, the mind needs food. We feed it each day for an hour and a half. That's all. That's the meaning of it.

okusan—
jabbering into your cellular phone
this windy day

Rushing water over stone creates a barely discernible roar, subtle but potent counterpoint to the creek's continuous gurgling. For the moment I don't read. The fire, the creek, the building group-concentration and my warmth (finally) fill me.

Christmas Eve
listen—
snow is falling

It annoys me to read about Buddhism. If I read at all, I want it to address Buddhism indirectly.

tiny ginkgo
releasing a torrent of rain
after the storm

I wrap an interesting book about the structure of Japanese houses in brown paper (to disguise it—in study period we are required to read about Buddhism). The same mind that designs the *ōryōki* designs living spaces, every detail of one's daily needs crafted into a feature of the architecture. The inclusivity is mesmerizing. I want to live my life this way. In fact this is why I am here, right now, painfully attending to the neglected (larger) implications contingent upon the extreme good fortune of being incarnated in a human body.

spanning the river
still faintly purling . . .
ribbons of moon

Fragile Limbs Nubbed with Blossoms

My dorm room is a tiny square. Beneath its window is a platform for my futon and there is just enough additional area for my desk, a shiny piece of redwood. Three lighted lanterns keep it toasty. I immediately picture myself reading without being cold, sleeping without being cold, sewing without being cold. It's also right next door to the *zendo*.

dawn:
"peep peep peep"—
through my airy curtains

Tassajara is about breathing, and by extension, the next level of care necessary for the body so that it can breathe—an allotted amount of sleep, three balanced meals, a bath, a period of study and rest from work every fifth day. Much attention is lavished on all aspects of these activities so that washing one's clothes takes its rightful place as a primary concern. One needs clothes for breathing. Therefore one must be prepared to sew or buy them, mend them, wash them, store them so that they stay clean and available.

fog rolls in
fat gulls
huddle over the water

On a sparkling day in March I rather enjoy the outdoor tubs, the sense of others also washing their clothes and then hanging them with pins on the long lines to dry in the sun. But on rainy or bitter-cold days it seems an endless process to schlep my dirty belongings up to the wash area, compete for a space to soak them, return in several hours for rinsing, and then schlep the now heavier load to the muddy field and fight for room on the clothesline.

plump, wobbly
chewing your way
through the rain-soaked leaves

The sun is warm and the afternoon air full of spring. I pull my chair toward a ginkgo tree, close to it but at an angle. Its fragile limbs nubbed with blossoms jut awkwardly as if each branch sprouts independently, full of intention, only later to learn it is in another's way. I can't take my eyes off it. It is so young.

indian summer:
Japanese girls giggle and
loudly suck their straws

Cooled Again by the Evening Breeze

A rather broad pathway links the tiny bath houses (one for men, one for women) to the main grounds. Beyond them are hills, meadows and wilderness.

moonrise—
beanstalks and melon vines
droop over the muddy road

One dresses for a bath (robe and zoris), brings along clean underwear and bathing accessories and allows five to eight minutes "travel time" in each direction. It takes planning and some deliberation to pad down the lane and maneuver the hump of the wooden bridge that arches over the creek.

starless night:
clawing up the slimy bank
a river crab

Embraced by the valley's quietness, the path is sprayed in a thin mist. I cross the bridge, *gassho* at the altar reciting the *gata* mentally, steel myself to undress in the freezing air, and step into the water. I pause, knee-deep, while my body adjusts to the heat. I step down one step and the water reaches my hips, then another and it rises to my waist. Then I squat so that I am totally immersed. I swim to the other side, turn around and look out at the mountains, the madrone trees, the rising sun, and listen to the whirling creek.

dawn
softly softly
through the undergrowth

The afternoon creek is lively. Turtles, snakes, bugs, butterflies, frogs, tadpoles, and wildflowers enshrine the slippery stones over which the water gushes. Removing one's shoes, walking barefoot to the other side of the overpass to the altar where one pauses (to dedicate the act of washing one's body to all sentient beings), gingerly one enters the open-air cubicles with their cement tubs.

mountain shrine:
fragrance from
an unknown place

Each rectangular tub holds two bathers. During the afternoon bath period there is not time to fill and empty them more than once, so women take turns soaping and rinsing off. Like the Japanese, they wash first and then, entirely clean, enter the plunge or steamroom.

high and still
on the milky horizon—
summer clouds

The plunge is maintained by an attendant at 110 degrees at all times. One graduates to its deepest parts allowing the water to seep up one's body as the steam enfolds the still-yet-above-surface portions. The serenity of the mountains and trees, birds and flowers sink in with the heat until quite suddenly one is saturated.

folding its wings
a moth comes to rest—
evening settles in

One leaves quickly, drying, partially dressing. The cold air slaps the mind which must emerge from its sated state carrying an even-keeled warmth to the evening's meditation practice.

leaving the pool
cooled again
by the evening breeze

The sun set hours ago but residual light lingers over our valley with its last vestiges of warmth. Birds chirp and a slight wind rustles through the trees. Though in five minutes the sun will have dipped beneath the horizon, right now it blooms an iridescent yellow through the wild grass. The hillsides are teeming. Chirp chirp. The sun sinks a fraction lower.

night falls
curtains flap
in the shallow breeze

I shut my eyes and listen to the throat-filled calls allowing the cool air to dry the beads of steam across my forehead. My kimono is loosely tied. A shallow breeze brushes my chest, spreads through the wide sleeves and around my thighs as the skirt balloons slightly. A strip of light falls on a wooden chair, ancient and peeling with blotches of white bird-droppings on its flared arms and angled center, the slabs weather-beaten. The sun momentarily hovers, sanctifying the chair, but is gone by the time I slowly pass, returning from the baths to my cabin to dress for dinner.

night falls
I watch—
door ajar

Acre After Acre After Acre
Explode in the Four Directions

A breathtaking day. Gold and red leaves shimmer against the sky, their fragility contrasting with the rugged mountainous air. We are seated in the *zendo* which runs along the creek, one by one shouting our question (the question designed to demonstrate our understanding) at the Roshi. The practice period is about to end.

the wind blows stronger—
old women rustle through
piles of free clothes

"Fire Fire!" someone bursts into the *zendo*. Several young men bow to their cushions, rolling up their sleeves (there's a way of tying up the voluptuous black sitting-robe sleeves when one wants to accomplish a daily-life task) as they depart, the gesture indicating, "We'll take care of this."

winds blow briskly this evening
crickets are beginning to chirp
tell me—blue jesus—
why do you pick now
to be silent

The fire roars like wind. Dirty grey air (oppressive air darker than fog so that it's eerie, unnatural) smirches the chilly morning with its stuffy presence. Deposits of ash, snow-like, invade every exposed surface. One gags on a drink of water.

a fledgling drinks . . .
insects float
on the stagnant swamp

Our routine, our sky, our beds, our baths—everything is polluted with the fire's residue.

hot windless day
even the song-sparrow's nest
is deserted

Chop chop chop. The carrot is now a row of paper-thin, salad-ready (they are too skinny for soup or mixed vegetables) slices. I am momentarily in control. Chopping block, *hocho* (knife) and me standing, cutting the decisive widths. I feel exhausted, but the wafer-size carrot wheels are perfect.

Bashō
your rainproof paper hat
made with your own hands
the one imitating Saigyō's . . .
I too have felt desperately alone

Our snug (albeit gritty) sense of placement in this valley is comical once one sees the firezone from an aeronautical perspective. Acre after acre after acre explode in the four directions, Tassajara a dot directly in its path.

snowstorm:
one tam-ó-shanter
dissolves into the flurry

Our tactic is to cut a trench around the monastery wide enough to stop the fire as it approaches. Fires need food. Trenches have none. Theoretically the fire will extinguish itself (if the wind cooperates). But the fire by now is so huge and so old. Self-consumption (as in the case of humans) could sustain it for a long time.

scorching
a no-longer-summer landscape—
summer heat

Frogs Wait, Birds Wait, Snakes Wait

After the fire, conditions at Tassajara become crowded what with the extra help brought in to clean and repair the damage. Three and four people are squished into a room. The hill cabin I am assigned is partitioned in two with (miraculously) only me in the front with a view of the entire valley.

after the storm
a cerulean sky—floods the banks
of the deep draw

The approach is up a narrow footpath through idyllic yellow grasses. Perched atop my futon I survey the creek, the foothills of the adjacent mountain, its timberline, peaks and the shadows cast upon them by the sun and moon and clouds. At my elevation pesky blue jays sound nostalgic.

Easter sunrise:
kneeling by the jonquils
in my breezy pew

Indeed, except for the bells, whose reverberations distance renders even more soul-stirring, community generated noises seem remote, quaint, picturesque.

cat's back arched
in the waxing moon . . .
wind whistles through the grasses

Whereas formerly my room, a glorified trunk, housed my belongings and served as a changing station (tool for the schedule), my present room is a container for me. My new perspective is not only geographical. It is emotional and psychological. I see the context for my desires and can tolerate being deprived with greater equanimity.

frogs wait, birds wait,
snakes wait . . .
the season shifts

The Wintry Thicket Lifeless

At Tassajara it rains. I have told the *tenken* I am sick and to please bring me hot water in a thermos, later, after breakfast. From my bed I hear the rain softly falling and the sound lulls me back to sleep. A band of moonlight criss-crosses my otherwise darkened cabin.

cooling the night with its plashing
I doze . . .
dream of its plashing

It pours. Clouds are black. Buckets of water descend through the thick sky. Early in the morning I am at my desk. The screen-door behind me is open so that I hear the rain, its steady flush of water. The downpour creates an echo on top of which I hear (1) wind blowing through the Eucalyptus trees (2) the drip drip drip of drainage from the eaves (3) sweet clear singing from a variety of birds, one in beats of three (hoot hoot hoot...hoot hoot hoot) (4) insects on the hill chirping, buzzing, alive and busy (5) a woodpecker and (6) the sound of steel pounding steel. A train whistle blows. Out on the bay a fog horn moans.

       your mournful call
       crosses my mind
       this wet cold morning

I sleep. I sleep deeply and soundly and when I wake the room is filled with muted light. I turn over on my back doubling my pillow underneath my head, arranging the hood of my sleeping bag around my neck snugly while I reflect, starring at the rafters, listening to the pitter-patter pitter-patter soaking the already saturated earth. A Scrub Jay caws. Another responds, caw caw caw, as if railing against the sour weather.

no chirps
no twitters
just rain

Sometimes the wake-up bell will ring, with its primitive and unmistakably firm ring, and I cannot get out of bed. I lay there in the dark, in the glorious warmth of my sleeping bag, feeling remote, reluctant to decide to be at this monastery. The desire to stay in bed, finally to sleep enough, to be warm, to reconsider my life is overwhelming.

hatched
but slow to uncoil
in the mild rain

Through this "sickness" my life emerges. First I "get" that I am sick, the vast extent of it. Then I recognize the tremendous energy that I bestow on the things I choose to do. I can't help but ask why I pour myself into sewing, for example, and sneak out of *zazen*, when it is *zazen* I have presumably come to Tassajara to practice.

full moon—facing it
knees braced
beneath my robe

The answer is evident in my hands. My hands write and sew with immaculate, single-minded passion, passion that is sure of itself, pulsating and ecstatic. In the *zendo* my hands freeze. All the contraptions I can devise to insulate them beneath my robes cannot prevent their stiffening numbness.

winds howl
snow mounts
the wintry thicket . . . lifeless

Fat White Grub in its Beak

Winter practice period ends with the telltale signs of spring. Mornings aren't quite so cold, there is more light, a scattering of wildflowers, and, occasionally, afternoon temperatures warranting short-sleeves (no bugs).

splash of yellow . . .
first crocus on the
mist-beaded turf

We poof the pillows, shake and air the quilts, polish the wood furniture, arrange flowers, check and doublecheck the lists of guest necessities—as part of entering the mind of one unaccustomed to monastic life. Our intensity might throw guests off, obscure instead of sharpen the inner space they come to reclaim.

storm over—
the fragrance of pine
in the clear-cut

Opening the gatehouse in itself is a ritual, contextualizing the transition from a purely interior focus to a focus which is primarily interior but now includes our impact upon (and our perception of our impact upon) others.

softly scudding clouds . . .
a gaggle of sightseers
points at the roving flock

At Tassajara the gatehouse is a wooden shack with a very old-fashioned (and temperamental) telephone. As gatehouse-keeper, I greet visitors outside, rarely dragging them into the dreary office. I give them a little map highlighting their cabin, the *zendo*, the dining room, the baths. I explain our guidelines on conserving water. Like a *bodhisattva*, my sole responsibility is to anticipate and address the requirements of others. It feels awkward, unnatural. I am too much of an introvert really to care.

reeking of the sea
facing the sea
fat white grub in its beak

Lime-Green Sulphurs
Mud-Puddle in the Canyon Dust

One holds out for so long then gives oneself over to a chain of events by which isolated segments of one's life unravel. The contents scramble. The life force, renewed, released, slowly reconstructs itself, as if one's karma metastasizes.

autumn leaves
lie quietly
in the sun

One day I have the following thought: "I have spent eleven years as a Zen student resisting everything. What would happen if I take all the energy that I put into resisting and use it for something positive?"

eaglet
ripping the soldier
free from the asphalt

From this seed I develop "yes practice." "Yes practice" means doing only those things that I say "yes" to with my whole body and mind. I will not get out of bed until there is something I want that much. (I have to find out if there is.) If there isn't, I will just die, but I am not going to pretend for another second.

shrouded in fog
a tiny dinosaur
inches toward dawn

Soon it occurs to me that I want to write. Whereas formerly I felt I needed a specified subject, now I think: "If I want to write, I'm going to write. I'm going to write a certain number of hours a day just like I go to *zazen* a certain number of hours a day. I will not worry about what I write. I will concern myself solely with attending my writing periods."

high noon
lime-green sulphurs
mud-puddle in the canyon dust

I am through with Zen Center. I need to define my own regime. Zen Center has had it with me anyway. I am told privately that unless my attitude changes, I will not be accepted for Fall Practice Period. Indeed, my attitude has changed but not in the direction that would pique my interest in Fall Practice Period.

after the storm
over the hill . . .
zigzagging

Gravid Nymph

Saying "yes" finally was like a birth. And, like most other births, it came after a long period of gestation characterized by saying "no" only the "no" was unconscious. Immersed in the fog of my unconscious "no," I failed to recognize my own authenticity.

tadpoles!
bug-eyed and squirmy
in their bracken-shaded mud

A predominant feature of this inauthenticity was a sense of impending doom. Initially it hovered around the dreaded unnamed seemingly unavoidable crisis one could feel swelling in my childhood household. The atmosphere of this swelling—forces at work that I didn't understand, the largeness of those forces (that they were way, way beyond me), my ensuing inertia and blankness, and the resulting compliance (compliance being a form of inertia)—infiltrated all my subsequent endeavors, until "yes practice" broke through the gridlock.

warming earth—
its scent
in an early-spring breeze

Likewise in college, my inability to think and to write perpetuated the sense of being stalked—that at any moment something cataclysmic might happen. Because I couldn't keep up.

a
falcon
circles
evermore
narrowly
down
through
the
desolate
sky

And again at Zen Center where my unacknowledged anorexia stuck out, it seemed only a matter of minutes till the scaffolding of my life would collapse.

gravid nymph
grasping a leaf
with your claw-like toes

Determining to say "yes" . . . making that a conscious act—housing the bits of emptiness and despair that belonged to me and then offering them to the universe—"Yes practice" meant claiming my life. "Yes practice" was the beginning of living my life as opposed to an ersatz life.

waving long legs
dragging itself through the widening split
in the pre-dawn light

SHIWASU
*the moon in which monks scurry
from house to house reading the sutrās*

Under Ice, Under Snow, a Gracile Wing

Before "yes practice," my efforts to heal the indescribable thing that was the matter with me consisted of a series of self-imposed traps.

even in his company
seeing his grey hair
I long for his company

My inner world was blank. Nothing sparkled except my boyfriend. When he left, I was desperate for another such object through which I could experience myself. I chose food. I discovered that restriction of food has the side-effect of heightened self-awareness.

her lengthening shadow
                    young girl
    at low tide

Though my body was lean, my spirit was corpulent. The tactic I picked to combat my numbness in itself became a thing to combat, distracting me from the feeling I was trying to address by choosing it in the first place.

behind the storm-window
latticed with ice . . .
dangling threadbare wings

Once I was walking home from school without vitality or joy. I knew it would take an act of will just to make it to the house. I happened to pass a grocery store which, for a flickering moment, offered a ray of hope. "But," I thought, "what can I get? The food in the store either has calories or it doesn't satisfy."

the flock recedes—
I wander home
in the gathering darkness

The extent to which anorexia was a trap dawned on me. If I ate, I realized, I'd lose everything. If I continued to not eat, my life was a mass of listlessness and despair. I lacked the strength to choose—possibly even to stay alive.

winter's end:
curled along the window's ledge
a brittle body

Buddhism, also an attempt to heal the unpindownable sense of vacuousness that pervaded my life, turned out to be another trap. I began sitting *zazen* because I had come to the end of the way of life to which my parents had brought me up. I needed a deeper path—to access a larger part of myself. I didn't know what this meant exactly. It wasn't formulated mentally. I was drawn to *zazen* however at an important turning point.

from broken shell
to clump of bluestem . . .
making a dash for it

I tried very hard to follow the schedule because I believed that I had finally found—consummate and unfathomable—a path that plumbed the core of my being. Despite the fact that it was difficult, I told myself that at least I was on the right track. If I could just exert a little more effort, a little more will, a little more self-discipline . . .

flat pink sea:
saffron wings
flutter over the prawn boat

Ironically, the vehemence behind my determination hooked me irretrievably into another tailspin (I can't do it and there's no other choice). As I focused my energies on adjusting to the community (this, I was assured over and over, is Zen practice—"Just follow the schedule," everyone said, "while you notice mentally the obstacles that arise for you"), I failed to notice my unmitigated sense of hollowness and despair.

slipping on the scree
her wings smeared
my fingers powdery

I likewise failed a third time. As a young girl I fell in love with Danny. I was certain that he was the man for me. I ignored my extreme inhibitions around him, my fear of him, the fact that he didn't really know me. I just knew I "loved" him. Even after our relationship ended, I proceeded for over twenty years to have eyes for no one else. "My man is unavailable yet no one else will do" puts me in the same sort of bind as "If I eat, I'll lose everything" and "I can't do Zen practice but no other path is authentic." In this manner I constructed an endless series of (boxes) containers (a kind of mothering) for myself and spent a major portion of my life stuck in them.

under ice
under snow
a gracile wing

The milieu of "yes practice" is movement. It includes ever-changing me. Doing only those things that I say "yes" to with my whole body and mind releases me minute by minute to become who I am.

from the prow of the ferry
watching them spin ever faster
over the bay

After I formally left Zen Center, I moved into a neighborhood apartment and for awhile continued to sit *zazen*. One day I had an interview with the Head Monk. He asked about my leave-taking and I carefully explained "yes practice." He said to me: "Until you say yes, you cannot practice Buddhism."

an arctic basks—
wings tilted toward
the salmon pink sky

Glossary

Anja. The *anja*, one of the Roshi's two personal assistants, takes care of matters pertaining to his space.

Clappers. The *taku* (clappers) are small pieces of hard wood approximately two by two by ten. They are held parallel and struck together making a sharp clack.

Doan. One of a small group of students whose job for the practice period is to attend to the monastery's "sound system" (including the bells and drums accompanying formal services) and to enforce the daily schedule.

Dokusan. A Soto Zen term for *sanzen*, a private interview with one's teacher.

Gassho. A Buddhist gesture of greeting, palms of hands placed together.

Gata. A short prayer.

Han. The *han* is a thick rectangular wooden board suspended by cords outside the zendo and struck with a wooden mallet. The resulting sound, hollow and sharp, creates a haunting echo.

Jisha. The *jisha,* one of the Roshi's two personal assistants, takes care of matters pertaining to his time.

Keisu. The *keisu* (gong) is a bronze bowl twelve or more inches high that is struck with a padded mallet to punctuate *sutrā*-chanting.

Kinhin. Kinhin is the continuation of the practice of *zazen* done between formal periods of seated *zazen*. It consists of very slow (half-steps) walking.

Mokugyō. The *mokugyō* (wooden fish) is a hollow wooden drum, quasi-spherical, and carved as a stylized fish. It sits on a pad on the floor where one of the *doans* strikes it with a mallet to regulate the tempo of *sutrā*-chanting.

Mudra. Symbolic hand gestures associated especially with tantric meditation practices.

Ōryōki. The *ōryōki* consists of three nested bowls, a packet of eating utensils (chopsticks, spoon and *setsu*), a cotton napkin and a wrapping cloth which also serves as a placemat. Each student is provided with an *ōryōki* and *ōryōki* instruction upon arrival at a monastery (otherwise one cannot eat in the *zendo*). Thereafter the *ōryōki* is in one's care.

Prajña Pāramitā Sutrā. Known as the "Heart *Sutrā*" the *Prajña Pāramitā Sutrā* is the classical condensation of the six-hundred-volume *Prajña Pāramitā* literature, translated into Chinese by Hsüan-tang in the seventh century.

Precepts. Guidelines for training in wholesome conduct to which a Buddhist commits voluntarily. There are five precepts for lay people: to refrain from killing, stealing, lying, sexual misconduct and intoxicants.

Rakusu. A monastic or lay biblike vestment, a miniature version of the *kesa* or priest robe.

Robe Chant. I wear the robe of liberation, the formless field of benefaction, the teachings of the Thatāgatha, saving all the many beings. This verse of the *rakusu* is recited at dawn when priests put on their *kesas* and lay people their *rakusus*. It is also chanted privately whenever these garments are donned. The *kesa* and *rakusu* are the robes of the Buddha, treated respectfully and worn on all religious occasions.

Seiza. Seiza is a traditional Japanese sitting posture wherein one's body rests on the knees and shins.

Sesshin. Zen Buddhist retreats are called *sesshin,* a Sino-Japanese term that means "to touch the mind." It is a period of intensive meditation practice.

Shijō. The *shijō* (Cease and Be Quiet) is about nine inches high and struck by a *doan* three times to signal the beginning of a period of *zazen*, twice to signal *kinhin*, and once to signal that another event is about to begin.

Skandhas. The five *skandhas* are "bundles" (forms of the world, sensation, perception, mental reaction and consciousness) that make up the self.

Soji. A period of community cleaning.

Sutrā. Discourses of the Buddha (literally "a thread on which jewels are strung"), loosely used to mean old Buddhist scriptures or scriptures to be chanted.

Tangaryo. A five-day period of practicing *zazen* continuously from early in the morning until late at night instead of the usual practice of walking meditation between designated forty-minute periods of *zazen*. This initiation stemmed from a tradition in Japan whereby a suppliant is asked to wait outside the monastery doors for an unspecified time before being allowed to request entry. The long wait was a test of the suppliant's sincerity.

Tathāgatha. Literally "thus gone," an epithet for a fully realized Buddha.

Teishō. The *dharma* presented by the Roshi in a public talk.

Tenken. The *tenken* is one of the *doans* whose rotating job is to take attendance in the *zendo* and check on the whereabouts/needs of anyone not present.

Tenzo. The head of a temple kitchen ("head cook").

Umpan. The *umpan* (Cloud Plate) is a bronze plate shaped like a fleur-de-lis. It hangs from cords in the kitchen and is struck with a hard wooden mallet to produce a clangorous sound signaling meals.

Zabutan. A square mat placed on a tatami as a base for a *zafu*, one's round meditation cushion.

Zazen: Zazen is the practice of sitting erect on cushions, on a low bench, or in a chair. In Soto Zen *zazen* is keyed to the breaths and takes the form either of counting them from one to ten or of *shikantaza* (sitting with no theme). In his book *The Practice of Perfection* Robert Aitken has the following to say about *zazen*: "*Zazen* is itself enlightenment—as Dogen Kigen Zenji never tired of saying. This means, in his words, that body and mind have dropped away and they continue to drop away endlessly. The self is forgotten and it continues to be forgotten more and more completely through all time. Any residue of self-centered conduct, speech, or thought is wiped away. Any residue of that wiping away is then wiped away and so on endlessly—each day more liberated, each day more joyous. There are milestones on the path, as the Buddha found under the Bodhi tree, but they are no more than milestones and are not any kind of ultimate consummation. Perfection is a process."

Zen. A Japanese Buddhist school concerned with directly realizing the true nature of one's mind.

Zendo. Zen meditation hall.

The Moon of the Swaying Buds
is set in Minion, a typeface designed by
Robert Slimbach in the spirit of the humanist
typefaces of fifteenth-century Venice; it was
released by Adobe Systems in 1990.
Cover design: Bryan Kring

www.ingramcontent.com/pod-product-compliance
Lightning Source LLC
Chambersburg PA
CBHW080527170426
43195CB00016B/2496